"Dave Alvin's writing goes far beyond the songs that we've come to know and love. His prose and poetry share that same beauty and painful grittiness that is his beloved California. Dave's work celebrates the human spirit, as rich and full of soul as the man himself."

– *Louie Perez, Los Lobos*

"Dave Alvin brings a uniquely brilliant combination of talents and interests to his musical creativity. His knowledge of music history and lore seems boundless, and his technical ability is far greater than we normally encounter in an artist of his rank. Dave's writing, playing and singing are suffused with tenderness and insight."

– *Jimmie Dale Gilmore, The Flatlanders*

"Dave Alvin is a national treasure. With his masterful guitar slinging and resonant vocals that reach in and shake your heart, Dave paints soulful portraits of the America that lives on the outskirts. His brilliant songcraft— mixing strands of folk, blues, country and rock—makes him the undeniable 'King of Americana.'"

– *Jim Morris, President, Pixar Animation Studios*

"Mr. Dave Alvin is a personal hero of mine. Yes, it's partially because of his raunchy rebel rousing guitar playing, sexy rumbling growl, and his dangerous wide-legged stance, but mainly because of his WORDS. To read this many of Dave's brilliant words in one place is like entering a riveting All-American rock & roll dream."

– *Pamela Des Barres,* New York Times *Best Selling Author*

"This book is a wonderful rockin' ride through everything of value that matters. Bravo Dave!"

– *Terry Allen, critically-acclaimed songwriter/sculptor*

"Dave Alvin is a fountain of rock n' roll inspiration—the king authentic highway bard of barrooms backrooms and ballrooms—telling the true story, song by song, of our generation in America - and he never kicked my dog!"

– *Peter Case, singer/songwriter*

"Dave Alvin is one of our best songwriters."

– American Songwriter *magazine*

NEW
HIGHWAY

NEW
HIGHWAY

SELECTED LYRICS, POEMS, PROSE, ESSAYS, EULOGIES AND BLUES

DAVE ALVIN

New Highway:
Selected Lyrics, Poems, Prose, Essays, Eulogies and Blues

Book production by Adept Content Solutions

Cover design by Patrick Crowley
Cover photo courtesy of Joe Murray
Back cover photo courtesy of Edward Colver

Library of Congress Cataloging-in-Publication Data available upon request.

Hardback ISBN: 9781947026919
Ebook ISBN: 9781947026902

First printing
Published by BMG

bmg.com
davealvin.net

For

Gerald Locklin
Poet, mentor, teacher, and friend
1941–2021

Lee Allen
Musician, mentor, teacher, and friend
1927–1994

Big Joe Turner
Vocalist, mentor, teacher, and friend
1911–1985

Gene Taylor
Musician, mentor, teacher, and friend
1952–2021

My parents:
Eleanor Nana Smith Alvin
of Reedley, California
1918–1984

and

Casimir Dominic Czyzewski Alvin
of South Bend, Indiana
1916–2000

The six people who taught me the most about
writing, music, the world, and empathy

CONTENTS

INTRODUCTION

One night at some show in some joint somewhere along our great interstate highway system, I was introducing a song of mine when someone in the audience shouted, "Are your songs autobiographical?" Without missing a beat, I answered, "All my songs are autobiographical. . . . They're not necessarily true, but they're all autobiographical." I'd never thought of or said that line before (though I've certainly used it many times since); it just slipped out of my mouth, fresh from my subconscious. The more I thought about it over time, the more I realized that while it made absolutely no sense, it also made perfect sense.

Recalling that moment of onstage banter is a way of explaining that this book of my selected lyrics, poems, essays, eulogies, and blues is not *meant* to be a memoir, but in a way, it truly is a "sort of" memoir. The song lyrics I've included all describe and capture, in greater or lesser detail, pieces of my personal life and viewpoints. The various music writings are efforts I've done over the years that explain my personal tales of the powerful effect that music—along with the people who create it, celebrate it, or sell it—has had on me and my development as a songwriter/musician from my childhood up to this moment as I write these words.

Since I started writing songs, my lyrics have been about heroes, losers, winners, the brokenhearted, the hopeful, the forgotten, the beloved, and, especially, everyday folks just trying to survive day to day, trapped between forces larger than themselves that they don't quite understand. My songs and poems are populated by celebrated or obscure historical figures, non-conformists, criminals, angels, liars, dreamers, deceivers, blues shouters, mad rock-and-rollers, honky-tonk weepers, confused lovers, picket line believers, skeptical waitresses, and other characters who have always fascinated me. These are people I've known throughout different parts of my life, or they're people I abstractly feel that I know. No matter who or what they're about, though, they're all a part of me. This is true for just about every songwriter, poet, or novelist. We all carry parts of these kinds of characters around inside of us, whether we care to acknowledge those sides of ourselves or not. As artists, though, we must accept our less attractive sides that we keep hidden from others—as well as the good, decent, exalted, and transcendental parts of ourselves. I doubt that Shakespeare (or whatever genius the feuding scholars may decide actually wrote those plays) ever killed off as many people in real life as he killed in his masterpieces. As Johnny Cash would tell you, he didn't really shoot "a man in Reno just to watch him die." But at some dark points in his life, I bet he thought about it.

A few of the song lyrics in this book are not quite the same words you may have heard on a recorded version of the song. The lyrics to most of my songs cannot be changed without losing the meaning or intent of the song, but I do consider other songs to be compositions still under construction. Through many years of performing my songs live with a variety of different musicians, I allow myself to play around with lyrics of certain songs as if I was still writing the song, continuing the search for the right word or perhaps adding a new phrase to flesh out the story. There are more songwriters than you may think who do this. My attitude is if I wrote it, I can mess it up—hopefully for the better.

Due to space limitations, I've not included every song I've written. I've tried to limit the songs chosen to the ones that I felt could stand on their own, lyrically or narratively, without the music. Sadly, this forced me to leave out a few of my sentimental favorites, and I apologize if I left out of one or two of yours. I've also included a few songs that I've recorded but that have either never been released for whatever reason (*e.g.* "Angel on Your Shoulder" and "Dixie Highway Blues" were meant for my *Blackjack David* album) or have yet to record and release (*e.g.* "Death Of The Last Stripper," written with Terry Allen and Jo Harvey Allen, who have cut and released a lovely version).

As for the essays, versions of some of these works were previously published in the *Los Angeles Times* and *Mix* magazine, while others originally appeared as liner notes for a variety of album releases and re-releases that are identified alongside their titles. In some cases, they're reprinted here as they originally appeared. In other cases, I've included early or revised drafts that shed additional light on my thoughts.

A few other selections here were first published in the poetry books *Nana, Big Joe and The Fourth of July*, as well as *Any Rough Times Are Now Behind You*.

This collection is also my tribute to the people who influenced me the most (and continue to do so), both as a musician and as a writer and songwriter. As a musician, the most important to me are the magnificent blues vocalist Big Joe Turner, the rhythm and blues tenor saxophonist Lee Allen, and my hometown boogie-woogie piano master Gene Taylor. They were mentors, friends, and creative partners with me and my brother Phil from the time we were teenagers, and we couldn't have asked for better or more forgiving and patient teachers. Sadly, each one has gone on to whatever awaits us all on the other side of this life, but not a day goes by when I don't miss them or use one of the many musical lessons and survival skills they taught me.

As a writer, I learned the most from three professors I studied with in my early twenties during my checkered college career at Long Beach State University. Though these excellent poets—Gerald Locklin, Richard Lee, and Elliot Fried—wrote their poems in very modern free-verse styles, in their classes they were quite strict teachers who stressed learning to write in the traditional poetic forms. Thanks to them, I learned about poetic meters, syllable counts, how to rhyme halfway decently, how to write Shakespearean and Petrarchan sonnets plus alexandrines, haikus, blank verse, etc. (Please don't ask me to perform any such literary shenanigans like that now.) When the joyous, if heavy, burden fell on me to become the songwriter for The Blasters, the blues-roots cover band that my brother and I started in 1979 (with Bill Bateman and John Bazz), all the traditional poetry lessons I'd learned from these masters became my roadmap through the world of songwriting. When I started seriously writing songs, I thought I could somehow mix the blues and roots music that I love with the modern, small-press poetry that I was exposed to by my teachers. And I still use their wise instructions every time I sit down to write a song, a poem, or a story. I must single out Gerald Locklin, though. He was perhaps the first teacher to ever take me somewhat seriously as a writer and to treat me as an artistic adult even though I may not have deserved such respect. Gerald and I were lifelong friends, but I could never thank him enough for the kindness and faith he had in me when I was young.

This collection is also a tribute to my parents, Cass and Nana Alvin. My mother was a divorced factory girl, and my father was a World War II veteran newly returned to the USA when they met in late 1940s California. Their shared blue-collar lives, their wartime experiences, their empathy for others, their love of family, friends, music, and laughter, their "pessimistic optimism" or "optimistic pessimism" (which one of these terms suited them best depended on their moods) deeply shaped and informed the worldviews of my brother, my sister Mary, and me. Paraphrasing what I wrote previously about my musical mentors, I couldn't have asked for better, more forgiving, or more patient parents.

Whatever is good in this book, whatever words may move and touch you, is because of all these amazing, generous, tough, funny, loving, and warm souls. Whatever is terrible in this book is entirely my fault.

PS:

I'll end with this little music business story. Many years ago, a then-successful record producer asked me if I had a "hit song" for a then-successful musical act he was producing. I sent him a song of mine that I thought was pretty good. After receiving a copy of my song, he called me to nicely tell me that he thought it was "one of the worst songs he had ever heard in his life." When I inquired what, in his esteemed opinion, made the song so terrible, he answered, "Dave, you write weird songs. I imagine a couple of them could be small hits for someone somewhere, but these lyrics are just too weird for my taste, and I bet they're too weird for everyone else as well." I sat speechless for a moment and then told him, "If you think my songs are too weird, do yourself and me a big favor and never, ever read any of my damn poems." Whether or not you think my lyrics and writings are weird, I sincerely hope you can find a bit of yourself in them and that they can help you find your way through our crazy and intense, yet sweet and beautiful world.

LEAVING A
POET'S FUNERAL

I was leaving a poet's funeral
When another poet ran up behind me.
He firmly grabbed my arm
And tried to twist me around.

I turned and glared at him.
I didn't recognize his face.

When he said his name, though,
I smiled half-heartedly.
I'd known him a little bit, decades earlier,
When I was a very young man
Back before I was writing songs,
Before I was playing music for a living,
Before the countless years of highways,
Motel rooms and one-night stands,
Back when my only gigs were the occasional
Pass the hat poetry readings,
Back when I thought I might be able to survive
Somehow financially writing free verse
For small independent presses.

"Hey, man," he said,
"I just wanted to ask you if you're still writing poetry?
In the old days you had some potential to be a decent poet."

I smiled, "Yeah, I still write poetry,
Except that now it rhymes and you can dance to it."

ASHGROVE
(A BLUES BASHER CONTEMPLATES
LIFE, LOVE, POLITICS, AND DEATH.)

When I was a young boy, I used to slip away
Down to the Ash Grove to hear the old bluesmen play
There was Big Joe and Lightnin' and Reverend Gary too
I'd sit and dream about doin' just what they could do

Now it's been thirty-some years since the Ash Grove burned down
And I'm out on this highway, travelin' town to town
Trying to make a living, trying to pay the rent
And trying to figure out where my life went

   I want to go back to the Ash Grove
   That's where I come from
   I want to go back to the Ash Grove
   That's where I belong

You don't have to go searching, pretend or put on any airs
'Cause the blues are gonna find you some day, somewhere
Now, my mother's gone, my father's gone, so many friends are gone
All the old blues men and blues women have all come and gone

But I'm still out on this highway, travelin' town to town
Settin' up my gear and then I tear it all down
Turnin' up my guitar, standin' up this stage
I'm just tryin' to raise ghosts up out of their graves

   I want to go back to the Ash Grove
   That's where I come from

I want to go back to the Ash Grove
That's where I belong

I can't say I've been all sinner; I can't say I've been all saint
I've done some good things and I've made some mistakes
I've been in and out of love, I've said words I regret
I've been drunk and I've been sober and I still smoke cigarettes
But I'm still out on this highway travelin' town to town
And the news on the radio just brings me down
It's all intolerance and fear, ignorance and lies
It's the same old story, I've heard it a thousand times
And it gets me thinkin', it gets me thinkin' of
Friends and lovers and how they come and go
Like look-a-like houses on the side of the road
Full of everyday people just tryin' to get ahead
Tryin' to find one good reason just to get out of bed
'Cause we all need somethin' just to get us through
So I'm gonna play the blues tonight 'cause that's just what I do

I'm goin' back to the Ash Grove
That's where I come from
I'm goin' back to the Ash Grove
That's where I belong

AMERICAN MUSIC
(A HIGH-VOLTAGE ODE TO OUR
GREATEST GIFT TO THE WORLD)

Well, a US soldier boy
On leave in West Berlin
No music there that rocks
Just a thousand violins
 They want to hear some American music
 American music, they want to hear that sound
 Right from the USA

Well, it can be sweet and lovely
It can be hard and mean
One thing's for sure
It's always on the scene
 They want to hear some American music
 American music, they want to hear that sound
 Right from the USA

Well, it's the howls from the desert
The screams from the slums
It's the Mississippi rollin'
To the beat of the drums
 They want to hear some American music
 American music, they want to hear that sound
 Right from the USA

We got the Louisiana boogie and the Delta blues
We got country swing and rockabilly too
We got jazz, country and western, and Chicago blues
It's the greatest music that you ever knew
It's American music, it's American music, it's American music
It's the greatest sound right from the USA

Well, a US soldier boy
Has to stop right in his tracks
When he hears that crazy beat
He turns and doubles back
   Because they're playin' American music
   American music, and the whole world
   Digs that sound from the USA

MEETING MR. PHILLIPS

My friend Sonny Burgess, the legendary 1950s Sun Records rockabilly singer, called me one afternoon in 2000. He told me was playing a private gig that night at some swanky hotel in Pasadena, California, and invited me to come and sit in for a few songs, explaining that it was just a get-together of some old friends jamming for fun.

Believing that it was a casual affair, I showed up a little late only to be hustled through the hotel's backdoor service entrance into a dark ballroom and directly onto the stage. Sonny was already singing with a band that included Sun Records stalwarts drummer D.J. Fontana and producer Cowboy Jack Clement. I didn't look at the audience at all but quickly and sheepishly plugged in my guitar and tried not to screw up too badly.

After a couple of tunes, Sonny asked his "old boss" to please come up and say a few words. I almost fainted when, out of the darkness, Sam Phillips, the founder, producer, and radical visionary behind Sun Records, stepped onto the stage. It was then that I looked around the ballroom and saw that it was full of well-dressed women and men sitting at banquet tables. Then I saw PBS banners hanging from the ceiling and realized this wasn't a jam session of old pals but a serious wrap party celebration for a soon-to-be broadcast PBS documentary on Sam Phillips and his contributions to American music and culture. Mr. Phillips said a few niceties about Sonny, Jack, and PBS, and then made a few self-deprecating jokes about himself before returning to his table. When he sat down, I couldn't help but notice that he was sitting directly in front of me. Sonny quickly kicked off another song while I was nervously thinking how many times in my life would Sam Phillips (the man who first discovered or recorded Elvis Presley, Howling Wolf, B.B. King, and Johnny Cash, among so many other titans) be sitting in front of me while I bashed on a guitar? I took a couple deep breaths, turned my amplifier up a little louder (much to Jack Clement's displeasure and Sonny's joy), and I went for the guitar jugular.

6

Through the rest of the set. I played every raw, rough, rocking Sun Records / Sam Phillips–approved guitar lick/style I knew from decades of soaking in scratchy old Sun 45s and albums. From Howling Wolf's early guitar aces Willie Johnson and Pat Hare, to Junior Parker's underrated axeman Floyd Murphy; from Jerry Lee's six-string comrade Roland Janes; to Presley's fingerpicking righthand man Scotty Moore; with sizable slabs of Earl Hooker, Little Milton, Carl Perkins, Billy Lee Riley, B.B. King, Luther Perkins, and every other blues and rockabilly player who walked through the doors of the Sun recording studio in 1950s Memphis thrown into the mix.

As I walked off the stage, Sam Phillips bolted from his table, followed me to the makeshift dressing room, and then grabbed me in a bear hug. "Goddamn, boy!" He shouted. "You were kicking my ass out there! I haven't heard guitar playing like that in 40 years. Where'd you learn to play like that? You gotta be from Memphis, right?"

I knew perfectly well that Sam Phillips had probably heard thousands of six-string hotrodders copping Sun Records guitar licks over the last 40 years, but the intensity of his declarations, the passion in his eyes, and his constant back slapping made his little generous lies seem truly sincere. Of course, I told him I'd learned it all from old Sun recordings that he'd produced and that, no, I wasn't from Memphis but from California.

When Sonny told him that I used to be in The Blasters, Sam exclaimed, "The Blasters? No kidding? You guys had that 'Marie Marie' song and that 'American Music' thing. Man, I loved The Blasters! You know, if I was still producing records, I would have loved to have produced the goddamn Blasters." Then he laughed, slapped my back again, and added, "I don't know if we would have sold very many copies, but we would have made some great damn records."

With those kind words from that wild, incredible man, I felt a certain part of my musical life was sweetly complete. The Blasters may not have sold millions of albums or ridden in limousines from our mansions to the bank, but Sam Phillips dug us, and that means the world to me. Thank you, Mr. Phillips. Along with every other blues-bashing rock and roller around the universe, I owe you more than I can ever repay.

JOHNNY OTIS:
AN APPRECIATION
ORIGINAL DRAFT OF A PIECE FOR THE *LOS ANGELES TIMES*, JANUARY 21, 2012

Johnny Otis was a pivotal figure in my brother Phil's and my early musical and socio-political education.

I was about 14 when we started following Johnny Otis and his band around from gig to gig in Southern California like Deadheads and Parrotheads would do years later for the Grateful Dead and Jimmy Buffet. He had a swinging and tight orchestra that impressed me so much I can still name most of the members from memory—Big Jim Wynn, baritone sax; Gene "The Mighty Flea" Connors, trombone; Preston Love, tenor sax; "Shoop" Bradshaw, bass; Paul Lagos, drums; while Johnny played piano and vibes, and of course, his prodigiously talented son Shuggie Otis was on guitar. The shows he put on were a consistently thrilling tribute to West Coast blues, R&B, and soul and a throwback to the chitlin' circuit multi-artist revues of decades before. Dressed in a worn yet sharp black tuxedo—his dark sunglasses seemingly permanently attached and sweat beading on his forehead—Mr. Otis led the band with a firm yet easygoing grip, shouting encouragement to singers like Big Joe Turner or Margie Evans and to musicians like T-Bone Walker and Eddie "Cleanhead" Vinson, while effortlessly guiding one song into the next like the true hipster professional he always was.

Mr. Otis was always nice and friendly to us little Alvin boys, and that meant the world to us (it still does). He was even interested in managing one of my brother's teenage blues bands way back when, but Phil wasn't ready to take that leap into the music world yet. Over 20 years later, I saw Johnny perform in Long Beach, and he walked right up and started talking to me as if no time had passed at all. I can't express how touched and honored I felt by that.

Johnny Otis was a gigantic force in R&B on the West Coast and in the Southwest as he gigged his path through the 1940s and 50s, from Central Avenue in Los Angeles to Houston, then Memphis and back to LA again. A case could even be made that Mr. Otis was as seminally important to the development and growth of rhythm and blues and rock and roll as Sun Records founder Sam Phillips or Chess Records co-founder Leonard Chess. Besides having his own classic hits with "Harlem Nocturne" and "Willie and The Hand Jive," Otis was also a record producer and talent scout. Artists like Esther Phillips, Wynonie Harris, Little Richard, Johnny Ace, Big Mama Thornton, and many more made their early recordings under the tutelage of Mr. Otis.

Not only was his music a big influence on me, his unique political and sociological views always forced me to think outside the box when it came to appreciating blues and R&B. Johnny Otis had a way of teaching those who cared to learn that the blues was not just a one-dimensional, feelgood party music. While this music could certainly get you out of your chair and dancing your troubles away, Mr. Otis would gently remind you that it was also an expression of the painful history of African Americans and other minorities in the United States and the constant struggle for equality, respect, and dignity. Johnny Otis made me think as I was rocking and rolling. Not many artists can do that.

With his passing, the golden era of wild, swinging, honking, and shouting rhythm and blues moves even further away from the glorious Central Avenue nightspots and the back-alley juke joints and deeper into dusty history books. Damn. This is really sad.

FLAT TOP JOINT
(A JUMP BLUES/ROCKABILLY FANTASY)

Down at the end of the freeway
Just behind some laundromat
There's a real gone little night spot
Just for real gone cats
It's called The Flat Top Joint
The Flat Top Joint

The band starts rockin' at midnight
Boy, you know you can't sit still
They got barbeque ribs, beer and wine
And sometimes, you know, there ain't no bill
Down at The Flat Top Joint
The Flat Top Joint

I'm gonna get my baby
Man, you know she ain't no square
But if you ain't got no honey
I bet you're gonna find one there
Down at The Flat Top Joint
The Flat Top Joint

You know, they got the best jukebox
Gene Vincent and Jerry Lee
Lightnin' Hopkins and Jimmy Reed
And the machine, it plays for free
Down at The Flat Top Joint
The Flat Top Joint

Well, the folks down there are friendly
But there just might be a fight
Well, a few broken chairs ain't no big deal
Don't worry it'll be all right
Down at The Flat Top Joint
The Flat Top Joint

GENE VINCENT'S LAST SHOW

It was Oldies But Goodies Night
At the Hollywood Palladium, July 31, 1971,
And the nameless back-up band started vamping
The grinding groove of
BE BOP A LULA.

Art Laboe, the border radio disc jockey,
Concert promoter and King of the Oldies But Goodies,
Introduced Gene Vincent.
The crowd cheered
As Gene ambled out on stage
Dragging his lame leg behind him.

I was fifteen
And had already seen Mr. Laboe
Bring out the standard Los Angeles oldies acts:

Bobby Day flew his "Rockin' Robin"
The Penguins crooned "Earth Angel"
Preston Epps pounded out "Bongo Rock"
While Rosie and The Originals broke old and young hearts
With "Angel Baby,"
And they were all fine

But this was Gene Vincent!
Yeah, Chuck Berry and Bo Diddley were still to come
And they would shake the Palladium's walls to the ground,
But this was Gene Vincent!

This was rare.
This was special.

He was already sweating in his leathers
Under the hot stage lights
As he grabbed the microphone stand
And started to sing
But it was clear that something wasn't right.

He was mumbling his words,
Trying to sing low, sexy and young.

Sing like he was still leading The Blue Caps
With Cliff Gallup's abstract guitar licks
Inspiring him to total rock and roll abandon,
Sing like he was still putting cigarettes out
On Johnny Burnette's arm,
Sing like he could before
The years of booze and obscurity,
Sing like he could before
The car accident in Britain
When he held Eddie Cochran
Dead in his arms.

But he couldn't.
The old fire wasn't there.
After a couple of perfunctory choruses of "Be Bop A Lula,"
Gene quit singing.
He motioned for the band to keep playing, though,
As a woman and three kids joined him on stage.
The woman put her arms around Gene
As the kids stood nervously around
His lame leg.

I couldn't tell if he was crying
Or if he was sweating from the stage lights,
As he said,
I'VE HAD A LOT OF HARD TIMES
BUT THANKS TO THE LOVE OF MY FAMILY HERE
MY HARD TIMES ARE IN THE PAST!

The crowd cheered.

AND I'M READY TO ROCK AGAIN!

The crowd screamed,
WELCOME BACK, GENE!
WE LOVE YOU, GENE!

Gene kissed his wife
And hugged his kids
Then they left the stage.

Gene Vincent died three months later.

In 1979, while recording the first Blasters album,
Rockin' Ronny Weiser told me
That the wife and kids were fakes.
Art Laboe had hired them for the night
Because Gene's real wife had divorced him
And taken the kids
Long before
His last show.

ROCK AND ROLL WILL STAND
(FOR THE GREAT HANK BALLARD AND HIS ROCKIN' MISS ANNIE)

There was a little night spot on the outskirts of town
The beer was cheap and the lights turned down
There was a boy on stage who could sing a little bit
Doing his versions of everybody's hits
He told himself someday he'd have a million fans
Everybody knows rock and roll will stand

A Hollywood agent finally caught the boy's act
Gave him a contract and slapped him on the back
"On the dotted line, please sign your name
You're gonna get a star on the Walk of Fame
Soon you'll have the biggest record in the land
Everybody knows rock and roll will stand"

  We'll clean up your act, take some more photos
  Everybody loves you the night of the show
  Annie's little baby has grown up to be a man
  And everybody knows rock and roll will stand

At a Hollywood club he gave his premier show
Some kids saw it from the very back row
The businessman said, "This is where it's at"
The kids said, "Man, we can do better than that"
They got some guitars and went off to start a band
Everybody knows rock and roll will stand

Well, there's a little night spot on the outskirts of town
Another short drop on the long way down
There's a man onstage who never knew when to quit
Telling everybody he almost had a hit
Now he's got a day job working with his hands
Everybody knows rock and roll will stand

We'll clean up your act, take some more photos
Everybody loves you the night of the show
Annie's little baby has grown up to be a man
And everybody knows Rock and Roll Will Stand

DO NOT PLAY THE BEAT
(AN APPRECIATION OF BO DIDDLEY)

"Whatever you do, do NOT play 'The Beat!'"

That was the first thing Bo Diddley said to us before we walked onto the stage of the Music Machine club in West LA for two sets in 1983. We were a mix of members of The Blasters and X who had agreed, with great enthusiasm, to back up one of our greatest heroes for free at a benefit show for the Southern California Blues Society.

To say that we were upset by his announcement (or warning) would be an understatement. How could you play Bo Diddley songs and not play the powerful, infectious, and sensual Bo Diddley beat?

Since Bo's first records for the Chess label back in the mid-50s, his "Beat" (a primal and relentless mix of the old "shave and a haircut" riff, Chicago blues grooves, and Latin rhythms) had been borrowed, stolen, or adapted by everyone—from Buddy Holly, to The Rolling Stones, to David Bowie—for their own hit records.

Now, even though Bo had used variations of the "Beat" over the course of his long career, he was asking us to abandon it entirely in favor of . . . what? It's sort of like asking an actor to do Hamlet but don't use any of Shakespeare's words. Blasters drummer Bill Bateman and X drummer DJ Bonebrake, sharing the drums and percussion duties for the night, asked Bo to clarify what beat they should play. He tapped out some rhythm that stressed a different accent, but to be honest, I couldn't tell what the difference was. Fortunately, Bill and DJ picked up on his instructions and, by the end of the first song, Bo seemed pretty happy.

It was a very good band, with Bill and DJ teaming for the essential duties on drums, timbales, and maracas, X's John Doe and Blasters bassist John Bazz sharing the bass position, while my brother Phil (who also played some harmonica) and I followed Bo as best we could on guitars.

Most of the songs in the first set were new songs that Bo had recorded but none of us had ever heard, let alone studied. We (and just about every musician in the modern age) had been dissecting all his old records for years with the passion theology students study the Dead Sea Scrolls or physicists ponder string theory. A couple of the songs in the set were straight blues that easily fell into a comfortable pocket, but the rest were extended, one-chord, semi-funk jams that wound up sounding as much like Bitches Brew-era Miles Davis as they did classic Chess Records era Bo Diddley.

As the set progressed, and I began to feel at ease with Bo's new beats, I started thinking that it was closed-minded of me to expect him to play the old songs in the same old way. Wasn't Bo Diddley as much of a musical revolutionary as Bob Dylan? Weren't his original recordings of "Mona" or "Who Do You Love" as unique, pivotal, and influential in their day as Dylan's recordings were a decade later? Maybe Bo wasn't the lyrical genius that Dylan is, but in rock and roll (or blues and folk), lyrics aren't necessarily everything. If Dylan could change the melodies, grooves, and even lyrics to his songs to keep exploring the possibilities of his art, why couldn't Bo Diddley?

Some people would argue that Bo Diddley was one of the architects of funk, and if that's the case, why shouldn't he be allowed to follow his own rhythmic path to wherever it might lead him? Why should Bo Diddley have to be stuck in the past just because that's where a part of his audience (and perhaps his backing bands) wanted him to remain?

I remember smiling on stage like a goofball as I realized all of this and came to the conclusion that if you really dig Bo Diddley, then let Bo Diddley be Bo Diddley! At the time, I was a young guy who was trying his best to replicate old music—and that's a great way to learn how to play, believe me—but that night Bo taught me a lesson about growing and surviving as a musician and artist: stay true to yourself.

After the first set I nervously approached Bo backstage and told him what I had been thinking while I played with him. "That's right," he said laughing. "I already made all them old records years ago. Now I'm keeping myself new." But, as we walked back on stage for the second set, Bo turned to us, smiled and said, "You know, you boys are pretty good, so I'll tell you what: The first song is gonna be 'Mona,' and you can play it with the Bo Diddley Beat." And so we did.

BOSS OF THE BLUES
(A BELOVED MENTOR PASSES ON HIS WISDOM)

I was 16 years old back in 1972
Cruisin' late one night down old Central Avenue
Just my brother and me with the Boss of the Blues
Now, Big Joe rode shotgun and I was in the backseat
While my brother drove us down that dark and empty street
Joe starin' out the window and takin' sips off his drink
He said "I've been to Kansas City, boys,
I've been to New York too
But there was no place on earth quite like Central Avenue
But to look at it now you won't believe it was true"

    "Yeah, we used to ball all night long
    We used to roll way past dawn
    Everything was jumpin' down on Central Avenue"
    Back when Big Joe Turner was the Boss of the Blues

Yeah, we passed burned-out buildings and abandoned stores
And Joe said, "Man, this ain't what it was like before
And none of my old friends are 'round here anymore.
Back then T-Bone was rockin' the Barrelhouse every night
And you could find sin, salvation, love, or a damn good fight
Yeah, I'll tell you boys, this was a poor man's paradise
Well, you see that vacant lot? That was the Club Alabam
Where I'd sing all night while Duke and his boys would jam
But no one 'round here remembers who the hell I am."

    "Yeah, we used to ball all night long
    We used to roll way past dawn
    Everything was jumpin' down on Central Avenue"
    Back when Big Joe Turner was the Boss of the Blues

Big Joe said, "Yeah, boys, we had a hell of time"
But then he stopped talkin' as the lonely streets passed by
He took a sip off his drink and wiped the tears from his eyes

"Yeah, we used to ball all night long
We used to roll way past dawn
Everything was jumpin' out on Central Avenue"
Back when Big Joe Turner was the Boss of the Blues

BIG JOE TURNER

Every juke joint
Every boogie woogie pianist
Every three-day rent party
And all-night saxophone battle
Every Kansas City black woman
California white woman
New Orleans creole woman
Every dress slit up the side
Every sweet barstool lie
And every bedroom glint in the eye
Every half-smoked pack of menthols
Every shot of whiskey
And every bottle of bourbon, vodka and gin
Every blues song
Every tapping foot
Every pair of shaking hips
Every song ever shouted from behind a Pendergast bar in wild KC
Or grinded out on a sweaty Central Avenue dance floor in old LA
Every riff ever swung with Count Basie
Every Chicago shuffle ever shouted with Elmore James
Every New York R&B chart bound rocker
And every empty gig on the outskirts of obscurity
Every Saturday night kiss
Every Sunday night tear
Everything that was good and right
Everything that made life worth living and struggling for
Everything that had love and compassion for the world
Is in a grave in Gardena.

LEE ALLEN

The cigarettes that killed you,
You can smoke all of them that you want
Now that you're in heaven.

Now that you're in heaven,
Each day of eternity will start in the afternoon
With a casual game of golf
Followed by an early evening recording session
With Little Richard or Professor Longhair
Or Fats Domino and Dave Bartholomew.
Of course, now that you're in heaven,
Every session pays triple scale
With generous royalty points
On the back end.

Now that you're immortal,
You'll have a gig every night
But only if you feel like playing.
The gig will be you and your tenor sax
Backed by a swinging, bluesy
Hammond organ trio
In an intimate, smokey nightclub
Full of amazing, smiling women
Of every size, age, shape and color.

In heaven there will be kids
Who idolize you, just like I do.
They'll sneak inside the nightclub,
Just like I did,

To learn how to look slick onstage,
To learn what notes not to play
To learn how to hold a cigarette with aloof style
And how to smile at the tough yet beautiful universe
When the music feels just right.

When it's time for you
To hit the bandstand in heaven
You'll stand up from your bar stool,
Set your scotch down on the bar
As a sweet black angel hands you your horn.

HOLLYWOOD BED
(SWEET TIMES ON CAHUENGA BLVD)

Lift up the shade, Let's see the lights
We came this far, honey, let's see the sights
Hold me close, don't try to fight
Let's work up a sweat on a summer night
Hey, hey, rockin' in our Hollywood bed

What's that you say? You've got a rich old man?
I live on the streets doin' the best I can
Now, he can call his friends, he can raise a fuss
He can call the cops but he won't find us
Hey, hey, rockin' in our Hollywood bed

Ooo, Ooo, Ooo, Ooo, Ooo, Ooo, Wee
Ooo, Ooo, Ooo, Ooo, Ooo, Ooo Wee
No need to cry, we're gettin' by
In our Hollywood bed

Tip the bottle slow, let's get real tight
The stores are closed 'til the morning's light
You and me, baby, never got what we could
Wastin' our time but it sure feels good
Hey, hey, hey, rockin' in our Hollywood bed

Ooo, Ooo, Ooo, Ooo, Ooo, Ooo, Wee
Ooo, Ooo, Ooo, Ooo, Ooo, Ooo Wee
No need to cry, we're gettin' by
In our Hollywood bed

JOHNNY ACE IS DEAD
(BLUES-NOIR NARRATIVE OF
AN UNKNOWABLE MYSTERY)

Down in Houston, Texas, on a Christmas night
With a gun in his hand and his name up in lights
He was young and handsome, the Prince of the Blues
In a sharkskin suit and alligator shoes
He was flirtin' with the women who had come backstage
And he said, "Ladies, want to see me play a wild little game?"
But Big Mama Thornton said, "Go sing your song
And put that damn gun down before somethin' goes wrong"

Big Mama cried, "Dear Lord," Big Mama said
He put a 0.22 pistol, right up to his head
Then he smiled at the ladies
And now Johnny Ace is dead

Well, the bandleader set his saxophone down
And said, "I think I better split before the cops come around"
While the crowd in the theater slowly drifted away
With their heads hung low, not sure of what to say
But slick Don Robey, the record company man,
With big diamond rings on both his hands,
Said, "I'm gonna send him back to Memphis in a refrigerated truck
'cause Johnny Ace is gonna make me a million bucks"

Yeah, Big Mama cried, "Dear Lord," Big Mama said
He put a 0.22 pistol right up to his head
Then he smiled at the ladies
Now Johnny Ace is dead

When Johnny came back home to Memphis, Tennessee,
Everyone on Beale Street came out to see
There were pimps and gamblers, husbands and wives,
And women young and old all came to say goodbye
As the choirs sang and the preachers prayed
Five thousand mourners marched him to his grave
Well, there may be a heaven and there may be a hell
No one knows for sure, but now Johnny Ace knows damn well

Big Mama cried, "Dear Lord," Big Mama said
He put a 0.22 pistol right up to his head
Then he smiled at the ladies
Now Johnny Ace is dead

BLACK SKY
(LOUD BLUES GRINDER)

Baby, black sky, black sky is all I see
Yeah, baby, black sky, black sky is all I see
Please stand beside me, baby
Shine your light for me

Well, I've been all around the world, ain't nothin' that I ain't seen
From the Mekong River to the San Joaquin
I made it down to Helena but it's just a ghost town
And I got to Jackson but they tore old Jackson down
Yeah, I've been around the world
Black sky is all I see
Why don't you stand beside me, baby,
Shine your light for me

Well, I went to the graveyard to see my friend one last time
People gathered 'round, some were praying, some were cryin'
They were talkin' about heaven and the final Judgement Day
But all I could do was say goodbye to him, turn and walk away
Yeah, I went to the graveyard
But black sky was all I could see
Please stand beside me, baby,
Shine your light for me

I wake up every morning and try the best I can
To make it one more day in a world I don't understand
Now the sun may be shining but there's darkness on the land
And I can't find my way, baby, unless you take my hand
Yeah, I wake up every morning, baby

Black sky is all I see
Please stand beside me, baby,
Shine your light for me
Yeah, black sky, black sky is all I see
Please shine your light pretty baby,
Take this black sky away from me

IN MEMORY OF ED PEARL,
1931–2021

I just heard that Ed Pearl, the visionary owner of the Ash Grove nightclub, passed away this last weekend. My brother Phil and I owe him more than we could ever repay. A generation of California roots music performers who grew up hanging out at the Ash Grove (folks like Ry Cooder, Taj Mahal, Bonnie Raitt, Jackson Browne, Hollywood Fats, Greg Leisz, Don Heffington, Bob Glaub, Jimmie Dale Gilmore, plus all the future members of The Blasters among many others) owe him that unpayable debt as well.

From 1958 until 1973, then-youngsters like us could sit at the feet of American music giants, hear their voices, study their fingers, listen to their life stories, and maybe talk to them (or pester them, to be perhaps more accurate). This precious opportunity also gave all of us the chance to learn not just about their musical techniques, but also to learn about the often tough, bleak, difficult worlds where their music came from. Because of Ed's passion for American roots music, we could soak in the hard-earned survival philosophies of these masters regarding playing music that was never quite commercially mainstream but was, nevertheless, as necessary as blood.

Thanks to Ed bringing in artists both famous and obscure, my brother and I were lucky (or blessed) to see near-mythical artists. From our early teenage years onward, we begged, borrowed, and cajoled rides to get the twenty-some miles from our hometown of Downey to the Ash Grove in Los Angeles to witness performances by Lightnin' Hopkins, Big Joe Turner, T-Bone Walker, Bukka White, Mance Lipscomb, Johnny "Guitar" Watson, Reverend Gary Davis, Freddie King, Big Momma Thornton, Fred McDowell, Willie Dixon, Muddy Waters, Juke Boy Bonner, Sonny Terry, Brownie McGhee, Clifton and Cleveland Chenier, Johnny Shines, Earl Hooker, Albert King, Johnny Otis, Eddie Vinson, Margie Evans, J.B. Hutto, Walter Horton, Junior Wells, Buddy Guy, Long Gone Miles, and so many more. Besides blues artists, Ed also showcased folk and bluegrass titans like Pete Seeger, Bill Monroe, The Stanley Brothers, Clarence White, and Ramblin' Jack Elliott, as well as beat poets, counterculture comedians, outsider actors, and radical politicians. Obviously, Ed's musical tastes cut a wide swath, and that helped me to see how these diverse musical styles and disciplines were all interrelated.

Due to Ed's unwavering social conscience, going to the Ash Grove was not just about having a good time. Whether or not you agreed or disagreed entirely with Ed's sometimes extreme politics (and many artists and audience members certainly did not), going to the Ash Grove was also about getting an education in the often dire, unfair, and unjust circumstances out of which our various beloved American folk musics arose. You couldn't separate the one from the other. At least not at the Ash Grove and definitely not with Ed.

Of course, there is no going back in time, but once this pandemic is over, I look forward to getting back on stage, plugging in my guitar, and raising some Ash Grove ghosts up out of their graves. It's the only way I can ever begin to pay back Ed Pearl and all the artists he made it possible for me to see when I was a kid. The music is still as necessary as blood.

NEW HIGHWAY
(HOPE SPRINGS ETERNAL BLUES)

Well I'm leaving this morning, baby,
Riding that new highway
Yeah, I'm leaving this morning, baby,
Ridin' that new highway
And the more you cry
The more you're gonna drive me away

I ain't got no family
Ain't got no wife or no child
I ain't got no family
Ain't got no wife, no child
Ain't got no religion
I'm just out here runnin' wild

Well, a rich man's got money
And a poor man's got his soul
Yeah, rich man's got his money, baby,
Poor boy only got his soul
I got this new highway
And I don't care where I go

Now this new highway, baby,
Takes me from town to town
Yeah, this new highway, baby,
Takes me from town to town
Where some sweet angel
Always lets me lay down

Now my Kansas City woman's
Got skin as white as snow
Yeah, my Kansas City baby's
Got skin as white as snow
My Deep Ellum woman's
Got hair as black as coal

But these lovers will leave you, baby,
Good friends will come and go
Yeah, your lovers will leave you, baby
Good friends'll come and go
But this new highway
Is the best friend I've ever known

Now the gold sun is settin', baby,
Silver moon on the rise
Yeah, the gold sun is settin', baby,
Silver moon is on the rise
Gonna ride this highway
'Til the day I die

DIXIE HIGHWAY BLUES
(SENTIMENTAL MOTEL ROOM BLUES)

Off the Dixie Highway south of the Virginia line
In a little motel room listenin' to the cars pass by
She said, "Hold me, baby, like you did when you were mine"

She came to see me after so many miles and years
Disappointments, misunderstandings and tears
But when I took her in my arms all of that just disappeared

And I held her tightly as the trucks howled by like the wind
And I started dreaming of how things might have been
If I'd have stayed with her and never made the highway my best friend

She whispered, "Baby, I'm sorry but I can't stay
You see, I've got a husband now and we've got a child on the way"
Then she kissed me goodbye just off the Dixie Highway

Off the Dixie Highway south of the Virginia line
I packed my suitcase and moved on one more time
'Cause now she chose her life and, Lord, you know, I chose mine

LONG WHITE CADILLAC
(SORROW AND REGRET IN A
1952 DETROIT SEDAN)

Night wolves moan, the winter hills are black
I'm all alone, sittin' in the back
Of a long white Cadillac

Train whistle cries, lost on its own track
I close my eyes, sittin' in the back
Of a long white Cadillac

One time I had all that I wanted
But it just slipped right through my hands
One time I sang away the sorrow
One time I took it like a man

Headlights shine, highway fades to black
It's my last ride, I ain't never comin' back
In a long white Cadillac

Sometimes I blame it on a woman
Why my achin' heart bleeds
Sometimes I blame it on the money
Sometimes I blame it on me

Train whistle cries, lost on this old track
I close my eyes, I ain't never comin' back
In a long white Cadillac
In a long white Cadillac
In a long white Cadillac
In a long white Cadillac

THE BLASTERS'
AMERICAN MUSIC
HIGHTONE REISSUE LINER NOTES

The Blasters owe a lot to a truck driver whose name I've forgotten.

In 1979, my brother Phil, Bill Bateman, John Bazz, and I were working day jobs, rehearsing at night in a factory in Garden Grove, and trying desperately to find any steady gig that paid more than free beer. Our friends, the great blues harmonica player James Harman and Mike Foresta, had recorded a demo tape of us, and we'd taken copies to every "cool" nightclub in the Hollywood / West LA area. Sadly, none of the clubs were interested in a roots rock band from un-hip Downey, California, with no in-crowd music scene connections.

After reading somewhere about "Rocking" Ronny Weiser and his small rockabilly label, Rollin' Rock, Phil called him about the possibility of recording us. Ronny was skeptical at first until Phil sang and played guitar for him over the phone. Within an hour we were sitting in Ronnie's living room playing him our demo tape. Ronny dug the tape but still wouldn't make a commitment to recording us. After all, we were completely unknown. We'd only played in biker bars or the occasional country joint on the decidedly untrendy southeast side of Los Angeles County. We'd yet to meet any of the Hollywood scenesters and tastemakers. There was no music industry buzz about a scrappy little blues/R&B/rockabilly combo tearing up the beat-up bars on the wrong side of Long Beach. We were nobodies from Nowheresville.

But then this truck driver came by Ronny's house to pick up some boxes of records that were stacked in the living room waiting to be shipped.

"Who's this playing?" The truck driver asked as he loaded boxes of albums onto his dolly. "This is my kind of music."

"It's us!" Phil said.

"Is this music on these records? If it is, I'll buy one right now. My wife and I dig this kind of stuff. We can't find music like this anymore."

We couldn't have asked for a better review even if we had paid him a million bucks.

After the truck driver left, Ronny quickly discussed how soon we could record, and within a month, we were in Ronny's garage/studio making our first album. James and Mike were with us for moral support, and of course, we drank a lot of beer. Phil, the most experienced of us, led us patiently and sang his young heart out. Ronny's German Shepherd pup Crystal barked through various takes (listen closely to "Crazy Baby"). James let me record with his white 1961 Fender Stratocaster that he swore once belonged to blues guitar giant Magic Sam. I made mistakes that I'll spend the rest of my life trying to forget, but the mistakes really didn't matter. The vibe was right and that was the most important part. Ronny kept pushing us to quit thinking too much and just keep rockin', and with a rhythm section like Bill and John, keeping things rockin' was no problem.

After that first day of recording, we drove back to our side of town, punching each other in excitement while shouting and jumping up and down in the car seats of my Chevy Impala like little boys. We yelled joyously at strangers in passing cars that we'd just made a record and we were going to be famous. I remember at one point that all four of us had our heads out the car windows, laughing, cursing, screaming, and howling at the moon.

Wherever you are and whoever you are, Mister Truck Driver, thanks man. The Blasters owe you big time.

TWO LUCKY BUMS
(BING AND BOB-STYLE SWING
DUET WITH CHRIS GAFFNEY)

DA: Two lucky bums doin' what we do
Sittin' in a bar and knockin' back a few
And takin' life as it comes
two lucky bums

CG: Ain't got much sense, ain't got much dough
Ain't too good lookin' but somehow, you know,
We've had our share of fun
two lucky bums

   CG: Been chasin' the same old dreams
   Down a road that never ends
   DA: And given the chance, old friend,
   CG + DA: I know we'd do it again

CG: We've got some blues, we've got some regrets
DA: Made some mistakes but nonetheless
CG + DA: When it's all said and done
We're two lucky bums

   CG: Been chasin' the same old dreams
   Down a road that never ends
   DA: And given the chance, old friend,
   CG + DA: I know we'd do it again

CG: Let's make a toast to the times we've had
DA: The good, the crazy, the rough, and the bad

CG + DA: We've survived every one
A couple of losers who won
And when it's all said and done
We're two lucky bums

Yeah, when it's all said and done
We're two lucky bums

1968
(OLD-TIME MODERN-DAY FOLK BALLAD)
DAVE ALVIN / CHRIS GAFFNEY

Johnny gave Joe his first cigarette
Joe lit the filter then he smoked the whole pack
Joe bought all the gas in Johnny's old Ford
And he always said that's what friends were for

Johnny married Tina, Joe married Dee
Two blonde-haired sisters from Covington, Kentucky
Then in '67 Johnny joined the Corps
Joe did too but he never knew what for

   Tonight in this barroom he's easing his pain
   He's thinkin' of someone but he won't say the name
   Folks say he's a hero but he'll tell you he ain't
   He left a hero in the jungle back in 1968

Johnny went from job to job tryin' to make ends meet
Tina divorced him back in '83
Now 30 years come, and 30 years go
And Johnny's got a grandkid that he barely knows

   Tonight in this barroom he's easing his pain
   He's thinkin' of someone but he won't say the name
   Folks say he's a hero but he'll tell you he ain't
   He left a hero in the jungle back in 1968

Dee calls Johnny every now and then
She talks about her children and her third husband
But when he asks about someone they used to know
Dee says, "Johnny that was so long ago"

Tonight in this barroom he's easing his pain
He's thinkin' of someone but he won't say the name
Folks say he's a hero but he'll tell you he ain't
He left a hero in the jungle back in 1968

SIX NIGHTS A WEEK
(SEMI-GREASY HONKY-TONK ROCKER)
DAVE ALVIN / CHRIS GAFFNEY

I've been singin' in this bar since God knows when, six nights a week
And I take off on Sunday, but then I come back again, six nights a week
Lookin' at the same old faces, countin' all the empty seats
Wishing you'd walk through that door, six nights a week

Well, Crazy Charlie wants the same old song, six nights a week
He puts a dollar in the tip jar and then he sings along, six nights a week
So, I do that one about a hotel at the end of a Lonely Street
And remember how you said goodbye, six nights a week

   Six nights a week from 9 until 2,
   Lord, what else in this world am I supposed to do?
   Countin' every night as my life slips away
   Lookin' for your face from the same damn stage

Lucille sits at the same bar stool, six nights a week
And she don't say nothin' until she's had quite a few, six nights a week
Then she tells me she can make me happy, and she says it with a smile and a wink
But at 2 am I'm goin' home alone, six nights a week

   Six nights a week from 9 until 2
   Lord, what else in the world am I supposed to do?
   Countin' every night as my life slips away
   Lookin' for your face from the same damn stage
   Six nights, six nights a week
   Six nights, six nights a week
   Yeah, six nights, six nights a week

NO WORRIES MIJA
(TENDER BORDERLAND BALLAD)
DAVE ALVIN / CHRIS GAFFNEY

No worries Mija, everything will be fine
I'm gonna make us some money doin' a drive 'cross the borderline
It's a favor for a friend and it shouldn't take much time
So no worries Mija, everything will be fine

No worries Mija 'cause I've done this job before
And it's probably for the best I don't tell you any more
But it won't be too long now, and I'll be standin' back at your door
So no worries Mija 'cause I've done this job before

No worries Mija, little one don't cry
Yeah, there may be some trouble, honey, I won't lie
But I would do anything to keep you by my side
So no worries Mija, little one don't cry

No worries Mija, everything will be fine
I'm gonna make us some money, now let me kiss you goodbye
And if anything should happen, please remember you'll always be mine
So no worries Mija, no worries Mija
No worries Mija, you will always be mine

RUN CONEJO RUN
(BO DIDDLEY-ISH BLUES-ROCKER
FOR CHRIS GAFFNEY)

The other kids called him Conejo 'cause he was fast on his feet
And he was quick with his fists if he had trouble in the streets
But when his old man would hit the bottle, he'd kick Conejo's ass
And with a wounded heart Conejo swore he'd outrun his past
Run, Conejo, run

He boxed lightweight at the Olympic, down in dirty old LA,
And he earned his Golden Gloves by putting 16 fighters away
But the 17th one nailed him and blinded his left eye
So with busted fingers and a battered brain, he kissed the ring goodbye
Run, Conejo, run; run, Conejo, run
Run through the dark night into the rising sun
Run, Conejo, run

He was singin' in a barroom on the night that we crossed paths
We'd known each other all our lives but finally met at last
And we ran these highways 20 years fueled by beer and nicotine
From New York to Nogales and every joint in between
Run, Conejo, run

Well, he told me his life story, his joys and his regrets
From the hot streets of Tucson to a cold prison in Quebec
From his ex-wives and old lovers and the promises they believed
To the daughter in Louisiana that he never wanted to leave
Run, Conejo, run; run, Conejo, run
Run through the dark night into the rising sun
Run, Conejo, run

Well, it's three hours past midnight and I'm drivin' Interstate 10
A hundred miles east of El Paso and I'm thinkin' of my old friend
Well, I know that I can't see you, but I can feel you by my side
So light up a cig, Conejo, and let's go for another ride
Run, Conejo, run; run, Conejo, run
Run through the dark night into the rising sun
Run, Conejo, run
Run, Conejo, run; run, Conejo, run
Run through that dark night into the rising sun
Run, Conejo, run

GAFFNEY HATES POETRY

After not speaking for several miles,
Gaffney took a long pull
From his tall can of Budweiser and said,

"You know what's bullshit?"

Gaffney was sitting shotgun
While I was driving the touring van east on Interstate 70,
Somewhere on the southern Great Plains
Between Amarillo and Oklahoma City.

He'd been in one of his occasional dark moods
Since we'd left Amarillo late that morning
And the long drive across the dull,
Flat prairie and farmland
Had only made it worse.

"No. What's bullshit?" I asked.

I knew bullshit could mean almost anything to Gaffney.
It could mean whatever he ate for breakfast
Or some politician he'd seen on TV
Or the Dodgers weak bullpen
Or some ex-girlfriend who'd dumped him in 1980.

Bullshit to Gaffney, though, could also mean
His drunk old man knocking the crap out of him
When he was a kid
Or his various lingering injuries

from playing high school football
Or his bad left eye blinded back in his teenage boxing days
Or the year he spent in a Canadian prison in the '70s
For defending his then-wife against a man
Assaulting her in a Toronto barroom
Or it could mean the death of his beloved mother
Or the unrelenting arthritis
Slowly crippling his guitar-playing hands.

Gaffney crushed the empty beer can
With one hand and said,
"Remember that poetry reading
You made me play with you years ago?"

"Yeah. I remember," I said.

"Well, that . . . was bullshit!"

He dropped the empty beer can into a plastic bag
On the floor next to his seat.
"What the hell do you mean it was bullshit?"
I kept my eyes straight ahead at the highway.
"I remember that you had a good time.
You only had to sing a few songs
And you got paid more than you make
Playing 3 sets at some shithole methamphetamine bar.
Plus there was all the free beer you could drink.
What more do you want?"

Gaffney pulled another can of beer
From the plastic bag.

"What more do I want?
That's a stupid fucking question."
Gaffney opened the can
And sat silently drinking his beer for a few minutes.

The vast sky and prairie ahead of us
Were fading from evening gray to black
As a red sun was slowly setting
In my rearview mirror.

I kept my eyes on the road
And didn't say anything
But I knew he was glaring at me.

Gaffney lit a cigarette
Then exhaled the first, thin cloud of smoke
And finally spoke,
"What more do I fucking want?
I'll tell you what more I want.
I want no more fucking poetry readings.
Is that too much to ask?"

"Yeah," I said, "It might be a bit too much to ask for.
Anyway, what the hell do you have against poetry readings?"

"Well, those people you read with that night,
They all thought they were so fucking cool
With all their pretentious spoken word bullshit."

"Oh, they were all right.
In fact, they were actually pretty good.
Trust me, I've seen a lot worse."

"Bullshit, Alvin." Gaffney said.

I glanced over at him and smiled.
"You write songs. What do you think songs are?
There's really little difference between songs and poems."

"Bullshit."

"Well, seeing how you feel that way,
I probably shouldn't tell you that years ago
I dedicated one of my poems to you."

"Yeah, you shouldn't have told me that," he said.
"I hate the idea of my name being anywhere
Near a goddamn poem."
He dropped his cigarette in to his now empty beer can.
"You really should ask my permission
Before you dedicate one of your damn poems to me."

"You can be certain that I'll never make that mistake again."

We didn't talk for several miles and that was fine with me.

The prairie was dark and cold
As we passed lonesome lights
From sporadic farmhouses
And the occasional bright, warm lights
Of all-night truck stops.

My thoughts moved on to other more immediate concerns.
Salaries and other bills to be paid, phone calls to return,
Songs to finish and how much further I had to drive
Before I could fall asleep in whatever motel room awaited me.

Gaffney eventually broke the silence.
"I wrote a poem once. Do you want to hear it?"

"Sure. I'd really like to hear it,"
I said just to be nice.

Gaffney waited a moment
Then he gently recited:

"Every night at 3 AM,
My cat, Wally Bear,
Howls in the hallway.
Why can't I?"

Then Gaffney grinned at me
For the first time in hours and said,
"Do I have your permission,
My dearest friend,
To dedicate that poem to you?"

"Of course, you have my permission.
I'd be honored and sincerely touched.
By the way, that's a pretty good little poem.
Did you ever write any others?"

Gaffney crushed his beer can
Then placed it into the plastic bag
And pulled out a new one.
"No, I never did write another poem.
I figured I had probably said everything
I had to say about my entire existence with that one.
And, besides that,"
He paused for a moment with a satisfied smile on his face,
"Everyone knows that Gaffney hates poetry."

FOURTH OF JULY IN THE DARK
(A POEM WRITTEN A YEAR BEFORE I
REALIZED IT COULD BE A SONG)

After work I'd go to her apartment.
Sometimes she'd have dinner ready
And everything would be fine.
Sometimes, though, she'd have all the lights out.
She would lay face down
On the living room floor,
Her arms covering her eyes.
In the dark.
No TV.
No radio.
No records.
Silence.
In the dark.

Some nights I'd lay next to her,
Not talking,
Digging my face into the carpet with her.
Some nights we'd fight,
Neither of us raising our faces from the floor.

Some nights I'd sit at the top of the stairs
Outside the apartment, smoking cigarettes
Because she didn't allow smoking inside.
On those nights
I'd eat Pup n' Taco for dinner on the stairs
And stare at the neighborhood.

It was a dead-end street
Of run down 1960s apartments
And two-story duplexes

With only three sickly palm trees on the block.
People parked their cars
On what little lawns they had
And everything in the neighborhood
Was coated with yellow shadows
From the orange security lights
Of the Coca-Cola bottling plant around the corner.

The white kids sat around their vans,
Drinking beer, listening to FM rock.
The Mexican kids sat on their porches
Drinking beer, listening to AM oldies but goodies.
And she was laying with her face to the floor
In the dark.

Two years before
She was living in a Northern California redwood forest,
Going to college, making ceramics,
Eating natural foods and writing poetry
But something drug her down here.
Drug her down
To a factory day job in northwest Long Beach.
Drug her down here
To her family who made her stay
In the apartment they still owned
But in a neighborhood they'd abandoned.
Drug her down to a chain-smoking boyfriend
Happy to make minimum wage as a bad cook.
Something drug her down to the floor.

On the Fourth of July,
The Mexican kids shot off fireworks in the street.
The white kids watched from the other side of the street.
I watched from the top of the stairs,
Smoking as she lay inside
On the floor
In the dark.

FOURTH OF JULY
(EXPLOSIONS AND SELF-AWARENESS)

She's waitin' for me when I get home from work
Oh, but things just ain't the same
She turns out the lights and she cries in the dark
And won't answer when I call her name

    And on the stairs I smoke a cigarette alone
    Mexican kids are shooting fireworks below
    Hey, baby, It's the Fourth Of July
    Hey, baby, It's the Fourth Of July
    It's the Fourth of July

She gives me her cheek, but I want her lips
And I don't have the strength to go
On the lost side of town in a dark apartment
We gave up tryin' so long ago

    And on the stairs I smoke a cigarette alone
    Mexican kids are shooting fireworks below
    Hey, baby, It's the Fourth Of July
    Hey, baby, It's the Fourth Of July

Whatever happened, I apologize
So dry your tears and, baby, walk outside
It's the Fourth of July

    On the stairs I smoke a cigarette alone
    Mexican kids are shootin' fireworks below
    Hey, baby, It's the Fourth Of July
    Hey, baby, It's the Fourth Of July
    We forgot all about the Fourth Of July
    Hey, baby

SIGNAL HILL BLUES
(MURKY URBAN BLUES GROOVE)

I met her in a Long Beach bar full of drunk old men
She said, "You look like a nice boy and I'm lookin' for a friend
'Cause I got a bottle in my purse, and I got some time to kill
And I can show you a good time up on the top of Signal Hill"

Well, I was just 23 and she was twice that as far as I could tell
But I drove her up the dark roads past the old oil wells
And when she put her hand on mine, I admit I felt a little thrill
So I parked the car up in the weeds at the top of Signal Hill

"Well, those things will kill you," she said reaching for my cigarette
Then she took a long slow drag until the filter was warm and wet
And she pulled her bottle out and said, "This will help ward off the chill"
And we drank that bottle dry real slow up on Signal Hill

She said, "I used to dance in Vegas. Trust me, honey, it's true.
I knew all the cops and entertainers, and even a senator or two
And if I could've stayed out of trouble, you know I'd be there still
Instead of sittin' in some stranger's car on the top of Signal Hill"

Well, after she passed out, I just stared down at the city lights
And thought of all the dreams and broken hearts lost in the night
And I listened to her breathin' soft and sweet like a child until
The sun rose cold and lonely on the top of Signal Hill

NO OTHER GIRL
(A GUILTY ROCKABILLY HEART
FACES THE MUSIC)

Sittin' in an all-night cafe,
Drunk half out of my mind
Down to my last cigarette
Tryin' to kill some time
I don't know why I do it
Spent the day at another girl's place
She'll know that when I open the door
She can see by the look on my face

Waiting for me, she's waiting for me
No other girl would take it
Another girl would just give in
Another girl would throw me out in the street
No other girl would take me back again

A trucker takes his hat off
He likes his coffee black
Soon I'll have to face the fact
She knows that I'll be back
A busboy speaks in Spanish
A waitress checks her hair
I've spent so many nights on the town
But she'd always be there

Waiting for me, she's waiting for me
No other girl would take it
Another girl would just give in
Another girl would throw me out in the street
No other girl would take me back again

I don't know why I do it
Someday she might be gone
I'll buy a new pack of cigarettes
I've been in this joint too long

Waiting for me, she's waiting for me
No other girl would take it
Another girl would just give in
Another girl would throw me out in the street
No other girl would take me back again

WANDA AND DUANE
(SUBURBAN CHUCK BERRY-ISH ROCKER)

Wanda met Duane in a local bar next to an industrial park
Duane didn't like the clothes that she wore but she felt real good in the dark
After a few dates they said, "Why wait?" and Wanda moved in to stay
Into Duane's apartment on the second floor next to the 605 Freeway

Yeah, they made love in the morning, love in the evening, and love in the afternoon
Oh, but all good things gotta come to an end, even in a warm bedroom
Duane got tired of hearin' her voice and Wanda got sick of his breath
And they never said a word when they went to sleep on opposite sides of the bed

  Yeah, ain't it a shame, but there ain't no one to blame
  'Cause love just slipped away and only the lovers remain
  Yeah, Lord, it's a shame but there's really no one to blame
  So the names have all been changed to protect Wanda and Duane

Wanda joined a gym but she never went 'cause it was just too far away
And Duane held the TV remote control and he smoked three packs a day
Wanda thought that undercover she might take a lover but, you know, she never did
And Duane fell in love with all the naked girls in the magazines that he hid

  Yeah, ain't it a shame, but there ain't no one to blame
  'Cause love just slipped away and only the lovers remain
  Yeah, Lord, it's a shame but there ain't no one to blame
  So the names have all been changed to protect Wanda and Duane

Wanda was lookin' out the front door at the trees blowin' in the wind
She said, "Maybe someday I'm gonna blow out this door and I won't blow
back again"
As Duane was lookin' out the bedroom window at the leaves fallin' from
the trees
He said, "Maybe someday I'll jump out this window and not say goodbye
when I leave"

Yeah, ain't it a shame, but there ain't no one to blame
Well love just slipped away and only the lovers remain
Yeah, Lord, it's a shame but there ain't no one to blame
So the names have all been changed to protect Wanda and Duane
Yeah, there's no one to blame so we changed our names
To Wanda and Duane

LITTLE HONEY
(JEALOUSLY AND CONFUSION = TROUBLE)
DAVE ALVIN / JOHN DOE

Little honey, are you goin' out tonight?
Little honey, I ain't lookin' for a fight
Little honey, I promise I won't get mad
If you tell me about a boyfriend that you have
Who lied last night,
Who made you sad
Who left you crying by the side of the road
Who left you crying to walk home all alone

Little honey, won't you please come over here
Little honey, see we gotta get somethin' clear
Little honey, if you don't answer me soon
You're comin' home tomorrow to an empty room
With the lights left on
And the door open wide
The windows broken and your picture smashed
The window broken and our bed covered in trash

I ain't lookin' for a fight
But little honey, are you goin' out tonight?
No, I ain't lookin' for a fight
But little honey, are you goin' out tonight?

Baby, you know I care
But what can I do?
Just sit here waitin' for some lights on the road
Sit here waitin' 'til you come home alone

Little honey, are you going out tonight?

Little honey . . .

Baby, I ain't lookin' for a fight

But little honey, are you goin' out tonight?

No, I ain't lookin' for a fight

But little honey, are you goin' out tonight?

No, I ain't lookin' for a fight

But little honey, are you goin' out tonight?

WHY DID SHE STAY WITH HIM?
(MID-TEMP CHICAGO SOUL GROOVE)

Why did she stay with him?
Is there something I missed?
Was it 'cause she was scared
Or was it how he kissed?
So why did she run to me
When he made her cry?
What was I supposed to say
To change her mind?
When every time she'd go back again
Oh, why did she stay with him?

Why did she stay with him?
What didn't I see?
Was I so wrong to think
She could ever leave him for me?
Is that the way love is?
Is it cruel and unfair?
Can it make my two eyes
See something that isn't there?
And could it make her just give in?
Oh, why did she stay with him?

Why did she stay?
Did I do something wrong?
Did I come off too weak
Or did I come on too strong?
Well, I guess I lose, I guess he wins
Oh, why did she stay with him?

Why did she stay?
How long until I forget
When I held her in my arms
And all the things that she said?
Will she think of me when she feels his skin?
Oh, why did she stay with him?
Oh, why did she stay with him?
Oh, why did she stay with him?

SO LONG BABY GOODBYE
(ULTRA-FAST RHYTHM AND
BLUES LIBERATION ANTHEM)

Well, I know
I've been foolin' myself too long
I'm never right but always wrong
Goodbye, baby, so long
And you know
You never let this thing catch on
You never let me be that strong
Goodbye, baby, so long

There was a cold wind blowin' on the night we met
Windows were rolled up tight
We both asked for somethin' we could never get
So now I'll do what's right

'Cause we know
None of us are gonna cry
It wasn't even worth a try
So long, baby, goodbye

There was a cold wind blowin' on the night we met
Leaves fell from the trees
We both asked for somethin' we could never get
Now, I'll be the one to leave

And we know
None of us are gonna cry
It wasn't even worth a try
So long, baby, goodbye

BLUES FOR MISS MERCY

I first saw Miss Mercy in 1970 at the Ash Grove. She made a grand entrance into the club, along with a couple of other fellow members of the legendary GTOs. Her future father-in-law, Johnny Otis, and future husband, Shuggie Otis, were jumping the blues onstage with Big Joe Turner and T-Bone Walker.

I was just a 14-year-old, music-loving innocent from the nowhere town of Downey, and I'd never seen anyone quite like her (or the other GTO women) up close before in my life. Miss Mercy was dressed in her unique fashion mix that seemed to tell her life story—a ratty-haired Haight-Ashbury exile draped in blues queen Bessie Smith's feathers and boas, with gypsy beatnik jewelry hanging down to a vintage Clara Bow/flapper dress, matched with tall, tight boots, long scarves, and thick eye makeup that befitted the Laurel Canyon muse of Frank Zappa that she was. I'd heard and read of the wild "Girls Together Outrageously" group and was excited to see her and the others in person. I thought that she must be a truly brave, bohemian soul who cared little about the closed-minded constraints and opinions of the then-more-conservative society, especially the ones of my hometown and school.

I saw Miss Mercy several more times back in the Ash Grove days but after that scene ended, I didn't see or hear about her for another 10 years. Our paths crossed again in 1980 in front of the Whiskey, after a Blasters gig there, when my brother Phil and I rescued her from a gang of skin-head bullies (who thought that punk rock was about strict uniforms, not free expression—Miss Mercy was always about free expression and not uniforms). After Phil and I got her safely into our Chevy Impala, her first words to us were, "Hey! I know who you are! You Blasters are those little Alvin boys from the Ash Grove. You remember me? I'm Miss Mercy!" We drove her home as she described the ups and downs of her life the previous 10 years in manic detail, from moving through various incarnations of various Hollywood music scenes, to becoming a mother, to hanging out and working with Teeny Hodges and others at Hi Records in Memphis during the Al Green era. Phil and I felt honored to be driving her to whatever place she was then calling home, and we were blessed to become her friends from then on.

Over the decades, Miss Mercy remained an inspiration, an unpredictable joy, and a trusted advisor to me in many ways. She didn't mince words. She told you exactly as she saw things, whether you wanted to hear it or not. I didn't always agree with her, especially her strange collection of conspiracy theories (except for her take on the murder of Sam Cooke), but if she said "Mister So And So" was a no-good crook, I found she was usually right. And Miss Mercy was usually right about music. She knew her blues and R&B from South Central LA to New Orleans and back. She personally knew immortals, from Esther Phillips, Johnny Guitar Watson, Etta James, and Sugarcane Harris to Hendrix, Arthur Lee, Zappa, and Gram Parsons. And she knew her little Alvin brothers. Every time I saw her, whether it was at my gigs at The Troubadour, The Belly-Up, the Grammy Museum, or the last time I saw her in 2019 at a small party at the home of her best friend Pamela Des Barres, I felt the same rush of excitement seeing Miss Mercy that I had felt when I was a 14-year-old kid at the Ash Grove. She was always a truly brave, slightly out of control, bohemian, wild soul (who could also be funny, opinionated, tender, and loving), which was exactly what I had imagined her to be those many years before.

I don't know what awaits all of us on the other side of this life, Miss Mercy, but whatever it is, I'll meet you there wherever the lights are low, couples are dancing slow, and the blues are blasting all night long.

FRANK ZAPPA AT THE ROXY
ESSAY FOR *THE ROXY*
PERFORMANCES BOXED SET

In 1973 I was a 17-year-old, smalltown misfit waiting in line outside the Roxy to see Frank Zappa and his latest incarnation of the Mothers of Invention. If someone had told me then that 9 years later, in 1982, I would meet Frank Zappa, on—of all places—the Isle of Capri, I would have never believed them. I'm not even sure if I believe it now.

Though he was a Southern California guy, Frank Zappa's larger-than-life aura as a musical genius and all-around know-it-all made it seem like he'd fallen to earth from some distant, more advanced galaxy, rather than rising from the Mojave Desert dirt of Lancaster. It was surreal to find myself making small talk with Zappa in the lobby of a swanky, five-star hotel on the Isle of Capri instead of at some taco joint in San Bernardino. We were all there to tape performances for an Italian TV show, and he was checking out of the hotel just as The Blasters and I were checking in. Due to the heat that day, Zappa was wearing white linen pants and a loose white shirt, while we Blasters, with our hair in slicked-back pompadours and leather jackets, looked like rejects from Zappa's Ruben and The Jets. We were nicely impressed that this cultural icon was kind enough to talk with five young, three-chord rockers from the southeast LA County blue-collar town of Downey.

I broke the ice by telling Zappa that we had a mutual friend, the East Los Angeles singer Ruben Guevara. He smiled and asked about Ruben, and then said, "You guys are The Blasters, huh? I've heard of you. You're all from Downey and Norwalk, right?" We nodded, and then he asked us what we thought of Europe. We told him that we'd never been to Europe before and, after over a month of touring there, we were really missing Mexican food and our hometown. "Yeah," said Zappa, with a touch of sarcasm in his voice, "There is something about the southeast side of LA County that's like no other place on Earth."

Zappa listened patiently as I babbled about the various times I'd seen him in concert when I was a kid, from the Shrine Auditorium, to the Santa Monica Civic, to UCLA's Pauly Pavilion, but when I mentioned the Roxy his eyes lit up. "You were at a Roxy show? So, what did you think?" Being nervous, I stammered out the simple, all-purpose answer of "Um, it was really great."

Now, 35 years after he asked me that question, here's the reply that I wish I would have given him.

I was (and still am) primarily a blues head, but I also dug all kinds of music, from early rock and roll and R&B, to doo wop and folk and country, to all forms of jazz and modern composers like Ives, Cage, and Stockhausen. I was always interested in Zappa because I heard elements of those styles in his music (with the possible exception of country). No matter how complicated or cerebral Zappa's compositions would get, I could always hear traces of Johnny "Guitar" Watson's gritty blues in Zappa's solos, or I could make out sweetly shattered doo wop melodies floating through his pieces like "Village of the Sun," his ode to the bleak high desert of his youth.

The Mothers that played the Roxy shows were, in many ways, my favorite edition of the band. While I will always have a tender spot in my heart for the more anarchic '60s Mothers of Invention (particularly the smooth, Jesse Belvin-inspired crooning of Ray Collins), the Roxy Mothers were, in contrast, an extremely tight, diverse, and multi-talented collection of musicians with other-worldly chops who could seemingly interpret whatever music Zappa threw at them. It was as if Zappa had finally found a band that could actually play his music as he had always heard it in his head.

In the early '70s, jazz-fusion was the rage, and the Roxy Mothers, thanks especially to keyboardist George Duke and drummers Chester Thompson and Ralph Humphrey, could play that hybrid form as well as or better than any of the fusion combos of the time. They could also throw down some greasy funk and then, a moment later, transform themselves into a twisted, atonal chamber orchestra. The powerhouse twin drumming of Humphrey and Thompson received rock solid support from bassist Tom Fowler, who cooly negotiated Zappa's abrupt chord and tempo changes while his brother Bruce flawlessly handled the intricate, intense Zappa melody lines on trombone. The saxophonist/vocalist Napoleon Murphy

Brock impressed me, not only with his skills with various sax styles (from free-jazzing Albert Ayler to honking Joe Houston), but with the chitlin' circuit soul and muscle he brought to his vocals and stage presence. The Roxy Mothers were a grand combination of high art, low art, masterful technique, and razor-sharp humor with a touch of wild abandon.

I was especially happy at that Roxy show to have an opportunity to watch, up close, the outstanding musician Ruth Underwood as she frantically yet expertly dashed from vibes to marimba to kettle drums and back again without dropping a beat or a mallet. Ms. Underwood's invaluable contributions brought back the unique and eclectic sonics of the Mother's Uncle Meat era that I'd been missing in later lineups of the band. I also have to sheepishly admit that I left the Roxy that night with a schoolboy crush on Ms. Underwood that has lasted throughout the years.

Leading this powerful orchestra, of course, was Zappa. If he wasn't playing solos on his red Gibson SG that veered from complex lyricism to earthy blues lines, he was intently conducting his musicians, or smiling at some horseplay between band members, or beaming proudly at his ensemble and what they were capable of performing. I studied his eyes and the subtle movements of his guitar, taking mental notes of how he directed the group with these sometimes small, sometimes large signals. This lesson is something I have made use of while leading bands throughout my career.

As the decades have passed, I regret not thanking Zappa in that hotel lobby on the Isle of Capri for everything he did for me and so many others like me. I wish I would have thanked him for the broad musical education he gave me, as well as the healthy skepticism he imparted that helped me survive with some sanity in our often-insane world. I would add that, as a kid growing up where and when I did, Zappa's music and lyrics helped me to define myself as a bit of an outsider and a searcher. I should've told him that, similar to Raymond Chandler's prose and Charles Bukowski's poetry, Zappa's words captured the Los Angeles of his time and place. His lyrics—with their frequent references to less-than-glamorous Southern California locations like the El Monte Legion Stadium, or his passing mention of my hometown's Cadillac dealer's slogan ("Where The Freeways Meet In Downey") in "Billy The Mountain"—gave the seemingly meaningless and endless sprawl of sunburnt California towns and cities crammed tightly together some touch of bohemian magic and artistic credibility.

The Beatles sang about England, Dylan sang about New York City, but Zappa (like Brian Wilson and Merle Haggard) sang about California. A strange, underground, twisted California, but California nonetheless.

I don't know if that was what Zappa was trying to do with his music. I don't know if Zappa would have truly cared what some kid from Downey with a pompadour thought about his show at the Roxy, or what I thought about him and his music overall. Maybe he would have dismissed me as being too saccharine, pedestrian, or sentimental. Or maybe not. Who knows? Either way, I still wish I would have said it.

A HEART THAT'S TRUEL
(IN APPRECIATION OF DOC POMUS
AND OTIS BLACKWELL)

Doc Pomus and I were at an impasse.

Neither Doc, undeniably one of the great
Pioneers of rock & roll/R&B songwriting,
Nor could I find the right rhyming word
For the last line of one of the songs we were writing together.

These were songs we'd been asked to co-write
By film director John Waters for a movie
He was about to begin shooting called Crybaby
(a slightly twisted tribute to 1950s low budget rock & roll movies).

I was in awe of Doc's lyrical talents
And his important place in pop music history,
So whenever he and I hit a creative wall while writing,
I'd bring up names from his past
(like our mutual hero and friend, Big Joe Turner)
Or I'd pester him with questions about writing classics like
"Lonely Avenue" for Ray Charles,
"Save The Last Dance for Me" by The Drifters,
"A Teenager in Love" for Dion and the Belmonts
Or "Little Sister" and "Viva Las Vegas" for Elvis.

I'd then happily listen to Doc spin incredible tales
From his wild old days until we felt ready to write again.

This time, though, was different.

This time we'd been stuck for over an hour
On the last word of the last couplet
Of the last verse of the last song we had to write
And Doc wasn't in the mood to tell old stories
And I wasn't in the mood to listen.

Doc and I sat silently for several minutes
Until one or the other blurted out a possible rhyme
Followed by the other saying it was either a word
We had already thrown out 30 minutes earlier
Or it was the worst possible rhyme ever suggested
By anyone in the entire history of songwriting.

Then, out of the blue, the perfect word came to me.

I threw my pencil down, jumped out of my chair,
Yelled, "Goddamn! I got it! It's…"
And then I said the perfect rhyming word
To end the line we'd been struggling with.

Doc quietly nodded his head.

He whispered the word a few times.

Then he whispered the whole verse to himself
While tapping out the metric beats with his pen.

"It's good." He finally said. "Not great, but really good.
A hell of a lot better than anything else we've come up with."

I slumped back down in my chair in relief.

The song was finally done
And there are few better feelings in the world
Than finishing a song.

For a sweet minute I rested my tired eyes and mind
Until Doc shouted, "Wait a second.
No. No. No. This won't do. It's not a true rhyme.
It's a damn nasal rhyme!
No great songwriter ever uses a nasal rhyme.
It's a lazy trick for hack amateurs."

Then he added gruffly, "Your word is out of our song."

"What are you talking about?" I said.
"Look, I know some pop music sticklers hate nasal rhymes
But guys like you and me who love the blues,
We know most blues songs are full of nasal rhymes.
And we're writing in the traditions of the blues
So we aren't bound to the same rules
That Broadway songwriters are."

"I'm not just talking about show tune writers," Doc said firmly.
"I'm talking about all great lyricists in any style.
You take a great rock & roll songwriter like Otis Blackwell,
He wasn't some Broadway elitist.
He was soaked in blues just like us
But in all the hits Otis Blackwell wrote,
He never, ever used a nasal rhyme.
You hear any nasal rhymes in "All Shook Up?"
In "Fever?" In "Great Balls of Fire?"
No. You do not."

After all the many volatile band disputes
Back when I was with The Blasters,
I was tired of arguing over words, melodies and music
And I especially didn't enjoy disagreeing
With a wise and beloved elder statesman of song
So I kind of shocked myself
When I calmly said without hesitation,
"Really? No nasal rhymes in any of his songs?

What about his Elvis song,
'Don't Be Cruel?'
'Don't be cruel to a heart that's truel?'"

Doc stared at me in silence
With no emotion in his eyes
And no emotion on his face
For an uncomfortable period of time.

I figured that Doc no longer saw me as a songwriting peer
But only as a disrespectful know-it-all punk amateur
Who had crossed a sacred line that should never be crossed.

I was about to apologize
When Doc smiled and grunted out a raspy laugh.
"Yeah, yeah. Okay. You're right. You got me.
But that's the only damn time Otis ever did it in a song.
And our song will be the only damn time
I'll ever use a nasal rhyme in a song."

Then he stuck out his hand to shake mine and said,
"Your word stays in our song, my friend!"

KING CRY BABY
(HILLBILLY BOP MEETS RHYTHM AND BLUES)
DAVE ALVIN / DOC POMUS

Well, one for all and all for one
And all we want is to have some fun
Squares beware of our property
Yeah, if you're lookin' to rumble, you're lookin' at me

'Cause I'm the king, (bg vocals—King Cry Baby)
'Cause I'm the king, (bg vocals—King Cry Baby)
Yeah, I'm the king, (bg vocals—King Cry Baby)
King Cry Baby with a tear in my eye
And if you mess with the king
You're gonna cry, baby
Cry, baby, cry, baby, cry, baby, cry

Well, I was born on the wrong side of the tracks
In the backseat of a stolen Cadillac
I had my first cigarette before I could walk
And I've been strummin' this guitar before I could talk

'Cause I'm the king, (bg vocals—King Cry Baby)
'Cause I'm the king, (bg vocals—King Cry Baby)
Yeah, I'm the king, (bg vocals—King Cry Baby)
King Cry Baby with a tear in my eye
And if you mess with the king
You're gonna cry, baby
Cry, baby, cry, baby, cry, baby, cry

Well, I'm a lonely king who needs a queen
Yeah, you're the sweetest hunk of sugar that I've ever seen
I ain't got a ring or a crown for you
But if I had your love I'd lose these cry baby blues

Queen vocal: Well, let people talk, I don't care
Let me prove to you, daddy, that I ain't no square
King vocal: You be my queen and I'll be your king
Yeah, but if you leave my hive you're gonna feel my sting

'Cause I'm the king (bg vocals—King Cry Baby)
Queen vocal: And I'm the queen (bg vocals—Queen Cry Baby)
Both vocals: King and Queen (bg vocals—King Cry Baby)
King vocal: King Cry Baby with my queen by my side
And if you mess with us, man, you're gonna cry, baby,
Cry, baby, cry, baby, cry

A MEETING WITH THE MAN
GRAMMY-NOMINATED ESSAY FOR RAY CHARLES'S
GENIUS & SOUL, THE 50TH ANNIVERSARY COLLECTION BOX SET, 1997

I rode in a freight elevator once with Ray Charles.

It was several years ago in San Francisco, where an odd variety of artists from Lou Rawls to Ed McMahon to George Burns to my band at the time, The Blasters, were performing at some beer company convention. The only other person in the elevator was Ray's road manager, who nodded his head silently as I got on. His serious, businesslike demeanor seemed to say, "That's right, kid. You're standing next to THE RAY CHARLES, and he doesn't care to hear or make any small talk because he's only here to sing "America the Beautiful," get paid, and split. So be cool and we'll let you ride with us, and you can tell your grandkids about it when you get old."

Awestruck, I stood staring at Ray, who was smiling and softly humming a melody to himself. I tried to think of something original to say, but what could I possibly tell him that he'd never heard before? "Gee, Mister Charles, I'm your biggest fan!" or "Hey, Brother Ray! What's shakin', baby?" I don't think so.

Maybe I could've told Ray about when I was 14 in 1970 and the corner drugstore was selling cutouts of his old ABC albums for 69 cents, and how I bought two or three a week until I owned them all. No, nobody wants to hear about their records being in cutout bins, but maybe I should've told him how much I learned about American music and songwriting from listening to his records and reading the writers' credits. How he made me see that the same tough, blue soul in a song written by Percy "the Poet of the Blues" Mayfield could be found in one by country singer Buck Owens or by Broadway's Harold Arlen. How, more than anyone else in the history of American pop music, he had bulldozed the walls separating blues, gospel, country, jazz, R&B, Tin Pan Alley, and show tunes (and what other artist could claim to have made records with jazz luminaries like Milt Jackson and Betty Carter, as well as country icons like George Jones and Willie Nelson, as well blues titans like Lowell Fulson and Guitar Slim, and the Queen of Soul, Aretha Franklin?). And he did it without changing his unique vocal style, which was based as much in the church as in the juke joint. Would he really care that I based my approach to songwriting on his eclectic philosophy and how much solace I got from his example when people tried to pin me down to playing or writing in only one style?

Did Ray Charles really need some stranger in an elevator telling him how much of a revolutionary he's been in a country so musically, culturally, and racially segregated? Or how his music represents everything many of us believe America is ideally supposed to be: openminded, compassionate, independent, adventurous—willing to explore the new without discarding what was good in the old. I just kept my mouth shut and listened to Ray's humming.

Should I have told him about driving my family and neighbors crazy on my student tenor sax, honking and screeching, trying to learn the alto sax intro to "(Night Time Is) The Right Time"? Maybe he'd relate to how I sat up until sunrise night after heartbroken adolescent night listening to "I Can't Stop Loving You" over and over after my first girlfriend dumped me? What difference would it make to him that when I turned 21 and walked into an air-conditioned bar on a miserably hot afternoon the first thing I did after buying my first legal drink was play his version of "Ruby" on the jukebox and make a silent toast to adulthood and to Ray for being there to initiate me?

The elevator doors opened and, before I'd said a word, Ray and his road manager were out the door. I followed them out, watching as they were immediately surrounded by smiling faces and outstretched hands, everyone saying things like "Mister Charles, I'm your biggest fan." I still kick myself for not saying anything to him, but I also like to think that Ray knows and understands what he's meant to me, what he's meant to all of us, and, oh yeah, I'll definitely tell my grandkids.

HARLAN COUNTY LINE
(MOODY LOUD BLUES ROCKER)

Another morning, another motel bed
Another city waitin' up ahead
Light another menthol to clear my mind
Of those memories I pretend to forget
'Cause I always want to live without regrets
But, yeah, I still think of her from time to time
And is she still livin' across
The Harlan County line

Now, when we met, we were both livin' far from home
Tryin' to get by and tired of being alone
For a moment I thought she was mine
'Cause she had voice I just wanted to believe
She said her mother was full-blood Cherokee
And her daddy was a union man down in the mines
Fightin' the good fight 'cross
The Harlan County line

People can be noble, or people can be cruel
They'll make you president, or they'll make you a fool
But she always treated me nice and kind
Until that day she left me on my own
Said there was trouble she had to handle back home
Then she gave me a number and said, "call anytime"
If I ever made it 'cross
The Harlan County line

Now the years disappear out on the highway
And I lost her number somewhere along the way
So, I'll say a little prayer that she's doin' fine
Another morning, another motel bed
Another city waitin' up ahead
And another small memory to leave behind
Somewhere 'cross
The Harlan County line

Across the Harlan County line

BARN BURNING
(HISTORY AND INJUSTICE COMBINATION BOOGIE)

There's a barn burning, baby
There's a barn burning, baby
No, I can't say who's to blame
There's a barn burning, baby
There's a barn burning, baby
No, I can't say who's to blame
No one knows who did it, baby
And you best not ask my name

You better close your windows,
You better close your windows,
Better stay right in your bed
You better close your window,
You better close your window,
Lock your door and stay in bed
'Cause there's a barn burning, baby
And they say somebody's dead

There's an evil in this land

Good man's in prison
A good man's in prison,
And a bad man runs free
Good man's in prison,
Good man's in prison
And a bad man runs free
There's a barn burning, baby
Best not say you spoke to me

'Cause there's an evil in this land

Yeah, the rich get richer
Yeah, the rich get richer
And the poor they just stay poor
Yeah, the rich get richer
The rich get richer
And the poor, they just stay poor
Oh, there's a barn burning, baby,
I guess you won't see me no more

Oh, there's an evil in this land
Yes, there's an evil in this land

There's a barn burning, baby
There's a barn burning, baby,
No, I can't say who's to blame

DARK NIGHT
(HOT, HUMID, OUTRAGED BLUES)

Hot air hangs like a dead man from a white oak tree
People sitting on porches, thinking how things used to be
   Dark night, it's a dark night
   Dark night, it's a dark night

The neighborhood was changing, strangers moving in
A new boy fell for a local girl when she made eyes at him
She was young and pretty, no stranger to other men
But windows were being locked at night and old lines drawn again
   I thought these things didn't matter anymore
   I thought all that blood had been shed long ago
   Dark night
   It's a dark night

He took her to the outskirts, he pledged his love to her
They thought it was their secret, but someone knew where they were
He held her so close, he asked about her dreams
When a bullet from a passing car made the young girl scream
   I thought these things didn't happen anymore
   I thought all that blood had been shed long ago
   Dark night, it's a dark night
   Dark night, it's a dark night

THE UNDERLYING MESSAGE, 2020

During the time my brother Phil and I spent
  As young boys following and learning from
African American musical giants
  (Like Big Joe Turner, Lee Allen,
Lightnin' Hopkins, Sonny Terry,
  And so many others),
The most important thing that we learned
  Wasn't how to hold a guitar or what notes to play.
It was this simple yet powerful truth:

The underlying message of the Blues is
  That Black Lives Matter
The underlying message of Jazz is
  That Black Lives Matter
The underlying message of Gospel is
  That Black Lives Matter
The underlying message of Rhythm & Blues is
  That Black Lives Matter
The underlying message of Rock & Roll is
  That Black Lives Matter
The underlying message of Soul, Funk and Hip Hop is
  That Black Lives Matter

This means Blues in all of its various forms
    From acoustic to electric, jump blues to slow blues
This means Jazz from early New Orleans to big band swing
    To bebop to cool modal to free Avant Garde
This means Spirituals and Gospel
    From Blind Willie Johnson to Reverend Thomas Dorsey
    To Sam Cooke and Mahalia Jackson
This means Rock & Roll
    From Little Richard to Chuck Berry
    To Jimi Hendrix to Prince

It's a simple, powerful truth
    If you love/play American Music in all it's permutations,
    Especially if you're white,
It's the truth, the reality, the message
    That you must know.

Black Lives Matter

RICH MAN'S TOWN
(HANDY TIPS FOR URBAN SURVIVAL)

As tough as you are
  Somebody's tougher
Strong as you are
  Somebody's stronger
But as weak as you are
  Somebody's weaker
When you're living in
  A rich man's town

Well, as high as you are
  Somebody's higher
Tall as you are
  Somebody's taller
But as low as you are
  Somebody's lower
When you're living in
  A rich man's town

In a rich man's town, in a rich man's town
People look you in the eye
But when they look in a rich man's town
No one sees you as you cry

'Cause as quick as you are
  Somebody's quicker
Sharp as you are
  Somebody's sharper
Slow as you are
  Somebody's slower
When you're living in
  A rich man's town

In a rich man's town, in a rich man's town
People fall like drops of rain
And when you fall in a rich man's town
Even God forgets your name

Now as much as you've got
  Somebody's got more
As much as you get
  Somebody gets more
But as much as you need
  Somebody needs more
When you're living in
  A rich man's town

In a rich man's town, in a rich man's town
  In a rich man's town, in a rich man's town
In a rich man's town, oh in a rich man's town
As poor as you are,
  Somebody's poorer
When you're living in
  A rich man's town

COMMON MAN
(ANGRY, SNARLING BLUES)

He wasn't born in a cabin
He never fought in a war
But he learned to smile and quote Abe Lincoln
And to get his foot in the door

He knows all your problems
He shares all of your dreams
When he laughs his wife laughs too
As they ride in their limousine

So wave the flag and take a stand
Stand in line to shake his hand
He's says he's your friend
A friend of the common man

He's got all the answers
The good days will be back soon
There's one more strike in a copper mine
And a hungry child in each classroom

So wave the flag and take a stand
Stand in line to shake his hand
He's says he's your friend
A friend of the common man

Everybody works day-to-day to get by
Every morning searching for a reason to try
Ain't he the friend of the common man

He wasn't born in a cabin
He never fought in a war
But he learned to smile and quote Abe Lincoln
And get his foot in the door

With one hand on the Bible
He swears he's only here to serve
While everyone says, for better or worse,
We get what we deserve

So wave the flag and take a stand
Stand in line to shake his hand
He's says he's your friend
A friend of the common man

PEACE POEM
(DA ADDENDUM TO WILLIE DIXON'S SONG, "PEACE")

You can make money
Or you can make time
You can make a decision
You can make up your mind
You can make a wish
You can make believe
You can make excuses
You can make an apology
You can make love
You can make mistakes
You can make a promise
Or you can make a clean break
You can make an enemy
Or you can make a friend
You can make trouble
Or you can make amends
You can make a killing
You can make a speech
But
It don't make sense
If you can't make peace

JUBILEE TRAIN
(A NEW NEW DEAL SONG FOR NEW TIMES)

Honest John was a dirt farmin' man
Worked every day of his life
The dust blew up and the bank shut him down
When he heard about a jubilee train
Heard about a jubilee train

Well, Broadway Eddie was an uptown man
Never worked a day in his life
The stocks crashed down and he was out in the cold
When he heard about a Jubilee Train
Heard about a Jubilee Train

    You could see the men in the Hoovervilles
    You could hear the poor women cry
    Get on board there's a New Deal coming
    Get on board there's a New Deal coming
    Heard about a jubilee train
    Heard about a jubilee train

Well, Betty Jean was a factory girl
Never had another job in her life
The factory closed down and she was walking the streets
When she heard about a jubilee train
Heard about a jubilee train

Hometown Jimmy was a family man
Lived for his children and his wife
Business fell off and he lined up for bread
When he heard about a jubilee train
Heard about a jubilee train

    You could see the men in the Hoovervilles
    You could hear the poor women cry
    Get on board there's a New Deal coming
    Get on board there's a New Deal coming
    Heard about a jubilee train
    Heard about a jubilee train

There's a young boy by the side of the tracks
Alone with the flag in his hand
He heard a train passed by years ago
He heard about a jubilee train
Heard about a jubilee train

    You could see the men in the Hoovervilles
    You could hear the poor women cry
    Get on board there's a New Deal coming
    Get on board there's a New Deal coming
    Heard about a jubilee train
    Heard about a jubilee train

MAN IN THE BED
(A SONG FOR MY FATHER)

The man in the bed isn't me
No, I slipped out the door and I'm runnin' free
Young and wild like I'll always be
No, the man in the bed isn't me

And these trembling hands, they're not mine
No, my hands are strong and steady all the time
They can swing a sledgehammer or soothe a baby that's cryin'
These trembling hands, they're not mine

Now, the nurse over there doesn't know
That I ain't some helpless old so-and-so
I could've broken her heart not that long ago
No, the nurse over there doesn't know

   That the man in the bed isn't me
   'Cause I slipped out the door and I'm runnin' free
   Young and wild like I'll always be
   The man in the bed isn't me

I'm the man I've always been
I'm the kid who rode the rails through the Great Depression
I fought in the big war and marched for the Union
Yeah, I'm the man I've always been

So don't believe what the doctors say
They're just makin' things up so they can get paid
Yeah, and it ain't me they're talkin' about anyway
So don't believe what the doctors say

Because the man in the Bed isn't me
Now I've slipped out the door and I'm finally free
Young and wild like I'll always be
No, the man in the bed isn't me
No, the man in the bed isn't me
No, the man in the bed isn't me

BROTHER ON THE LINE
(COMPANY TOWN FOLK BALLAD)

Brother, the night's as cold on me as it is on you
And times are as hard on me as they are on you
There's a full moon tonight, on this factory it shines,
And you want to pass me by
While I'm standing on the line

Brother, I'm sure you've got the same dreams that I do
And we both tell ourselves that they might come true
But you see the men with badges, they say I'll commit a crime
If I don't let you pass me
While I'm standing on the line

Brother, we grew up together
Didn't we have some good times?
Two hometown boys forever
Now you want to pass me by
You want to pass me by

Brother, I'm fightin' for you as well as me
I gave 'em all my sweat; they want my dignity
So when the boss man shakes your hand and says, "Son, you'll do just fine"
And you walk into that factory to a job that once was mine
Well, don't forget your brother
Who's still standing on the line

GARY, INDIANA, 1959
(HEAVY POST-INDUSTRIAL BLUES)

I'm old, weak and gray and I'm runnin' out of time
Yeah, but you should've seen me, brother,
When I was young and in my prime
Back in Gary, Indiana, in 1959

I was a steelworking man with two kids and a loving wife
And the union was strong
Smokestacks burnin' day and night
Back in Gary, Indiana, in 1959

But then the accountants and lawyers and the bosses at US Steel
Sent down the word we had to take their rotten deal
But from Birmingham to Pueblo, Oakland to Allentown
The workers got together and we shut the big boys down
Yeah, the President and Supreme Court tried to force us off the line
Back in Gary, Indiana, in 1959

Well, 50 years disappear in the blink of an eye
And I feel like I'm a stranger in a world that isn't mine
My dear wife died; my kids all moved away
'Cause there ain't nothin' around here to make 'em want to stay
'Cause the factories are in ruins, decent jobs are hard to find
And you can't get ahead no matter how hard you try
Because the big boys make the rules, tough luck for everyone else
And out on the streets, brother, it's every man for himself
But I still remember when we marched side-by-side
Back in Gary, Indiana, in 1959

Don't bury my body, brother, when it's my time to die
Just throw me in that smelter and let my ashes fly
Back home to Gary, Indiana, 1959
Back to Gary, Indiana, in 1959

BOOMTOWN
(FAST AND DESPERATE BLUES)

Boomtown, boomtown
Better be careful, hard times in this boomtown

Skyscrapers rising from the desert floor
Eighteen people livin' in a shack next door
It ain't so easy livin' in this boomtown

They said the highways
Were paved with gold
But the concrete's hard and the bright lights cold
It ain't so easy livin' in this boomtown

Boomtown, boomtown
Better be careful, hard times in this boomtown

Everyday it's the same old thing
Strangers come to see what luck will bring
To boomtown, boomtown
Better be careful, hard times in this boomtown

They're building houses out on the outskirts
There's folks in town who can't get work
It ain't so easy livin' in this boomtown

Everyday it's the same old thing
Strangers come to see what luck will bring
To boomtown, boomtown
Better be careful, hard times in this boomtown

Skyscrapers rising from the desert floor
Eighteen people hangin'; 'round the liquor store
And someone said they heard about a new Boomtown

Boomtown, boomtown
Better be careful, hard times in this boomtown

TROUBLE BOUND
(EXISTENTIALIST ROCKABILLY)

Well, I'm old enough to know the score
But I'm young enough to want more, more, more
They say it means nothin' all said and done
But that's all right I'm just here for the fun
And I don't think twice when the sun goes down
I'm trouble bound

There's a demon deep inside of me
And sometimes I let the old boy run free
Tryin' to make a living during the day
But deep in the night I throw it all away
And I don't think twice when the sun goes down
I'm trouble bound

You see that girl looking fine, fine, fine
I'm gonna throw her a good time line
If she bites I'll reel her in
But if she don't, I'll throw my line again

Yeah, I'm old enough to know the score
But I'm young enough to want more, more, more
And I don't think twice when the sun goes down
I'm trouble bound

You see that girl looking fine, fine, fine
I'm gonna throw her a good time line
If she bites I'll reel her in
But if she don't, I'll throw my line again

Yeah, This old world is a tired place
It's the same sad story on every face
I'm tryin' to make a living during the day
But deep in the night I throw it all away
And I don't think twice when the sun goes down
I'm trouble bound
No, I don't think twice when the sun goes down
I'm trouble bound

OUT OF CONTROL
(MODERN DAY BLUES FOR THE INLAND EMPIRE)

I scored some speed in San Bernadino so me and baby could get a little bump
Now she's in that motel room puttin' on a show for some chump
Yeah, well baby's gotta make a living and I don't mind waiting out in the car
'Cause I got some nine-millimeter muscle in case things go too far
You know I try to take it easy, man, and just go with the flow
But sometimes things can get a little bit out of control

Well, my old man worked his whole life in the Kaiser Steel slag pit
And I worked there for a while back when I was a kid, but I got tired of all that shit
But that was years ago, man, before they tore that Fontana plant down
And my old man smoked himself into a six-foot hole in the ground
And I've got the same bad habit and it'll probably take its toll
But sometimes it's the only thing that keeps me from goin' out of control

Yeah, my ex-wife's workin' evenings at a Sizzler makin' minimum wage
And she's cleanin' up other peoples' houses every day just like some slave
And she's livin' with her kids in a mobile home just off the 60 Freeway
Some nights I go to see her and sometimes she lets me stay
Since she found Jesus, she's always tryin' to save my soul
But every now and then she still likes to get a little out of control

Well, I used to work a little construction, but I never got along with my boss
So I do a little import/export makin' enough just to cover my costs
And I'm losin' my hair and I'm losin' my teeth but I'm tryin' to keep my grip
To live to see one more day without makin' any stupid slips
You know, I could have played their game, man, and just done what I was told
But I guess I was born just a little bit out of control

When baby gets done in there, I'm gonna take her for a little ride
Cruise up into the mountains, park the car and get a little high
'Cause baby likes to look at the shootin' stars and make wishes as they fly by
And I like lookin' down at the city from way up there in the sky
And then I'll pull baby close to me when it starts gettin' cold
Close my eyes for a little while and let the world spin out of control

THIRTY DOLLAR ROOM
(EXISTENTIALIST URBAN BLUES SHUFFLE)
DAVE ALVIN / D. AMY

In a thirty-dollar room next to the airport
I can hear them jets through the night
Some people leaving, some people comin' home
There's a sign on the door says "Check out's eleven"
And a woman's earring layin' on the table
She said she'd be back, but I get the feelin' she's gone

   So I tell myself, one way or another,
   If she don't come back, there'll just be some other
   Who'll believe for a while I can promise the moon
   Shining through the window of a thirty-dollar room

Yeah, smoking cigarettes down to the filter
'Cause the pack's runnin' low and I don't feel like walking
Outside tonight, don't feel like anything at all
Lookin' around the room and wonderin' who's slept here
And where they were goin' and what they were thinkin'
Starin' all night long at these same four walls

   So I tell myself, one way or another,
   When someone moves on, there'll just be some other
   Who'll believe for a while they can promise the moon
   Shining through the window of a thirty-dollar room

In a thirty-dollar room, next to the airport
I can hear them jets through the night
Some people leavin', some people comin' home

So I tell myself, one way or another,
If it ain't this town, I'll move to some other
Where I'll believe for a while that I can promise the moon
Shinin' through the window of a thirty-dollar room
Yeah, shinin' through the window of a thirty-dollar room

BLUE SHADOWS
(HOME SWEET HOME FOR THE HARD LIVERS)

I've been around the world and every man bleeds the same
But when the lights are dim, you never know who's to blame
   I don't want no scars to show
   I don't want no one to know
   So, I'll be killin' time in the blue shadows

     No other place for me to go
     No other place for dyin' slow
     So I'll be killin' time in the blue shadows

I've been around the world, I'll take credit for the things I've done
But when the lights are dim, I'm not the only guilty one
   I don't want no scars to show
   I don't want no one to know
   So I'll be killing time in the blue shadows

I've been around the world and every story ends the same
But when the lights are dim, you won't remember my name
   I don't want no scars to show
   I don't want no one to know
   So I'll be killin' time in the blue shadows

     No other place for me to go
     No other place for dyin' slow
     So I'll be killin' time in the blue shadows

     No other place for me to go
     No other place for dyin' slow
     So I'll be killin' time
     Just killin' time
     So I'll be killin' time in the blue shadows

INTERSTATE CITY
(JUMPING AT SHADOWS HIGHWAY NOIR)

The cowboy checks in around midnight
   Into room number 503
Of the Best Western motel and truck stop
   Out on Interstate Highway 15
And he leaves a message at the front desk
   "When my woman comes send her up to me"
Then he sits in the dark drinkin' bourbon
   And he kicks a hole in the TV screen

Now the girl workin' down at the front desk
   Sits listenin' to the trucks drive past
And she stares at her pale reflection
   In the thick bullet-proof glass
And she thinks that her life might be better
   If she could change the color of her hair
And she remembers a boy she knew one time
   Who swore he'd get her out of here

    Come on, baby, take a ride with me
    Where the bright lights shine so pretty
    We can spend the rest of our lives
    Drivin' on Interstate City

Well now the woman pulls up to the motel
   In a beat-up Japanese car
Tryin' to figure out how that cowboy
   Tracked her down to the topless bar
And it's been so long since she's seen him

She doesn't know exactly what to say
So she lets out a sigh and tries to decide
   To go upstairs or just drive away

     Come on, baby, take a ride with me
     Where the bright lights shine so pretty
     We can spend the rest of our lives
     Drivin' on Interstate City

Well the state trooper turns off his headlights
   Runs a check on a license plate
He wishes he had time to call his wife
   To tell her he'd be workin' late
Then he checks with the girl at the front desk
   And he tells her about the APB
And he tries not to think of his children
   As he walks the stairs to room number 503

     Come on, baby, take a ride with me
     Where the bright lights shine so pretty
     We can spend the rest of our lives
     Drivin' on Interstate City

BEAUTIFUL CITY 'CROSS THE RIVER
(SMALL TIME LOSER'S REDEMPTION)

Bless me, Father, for I have sinned
My last confession was, well, God knows when
I'm a thief and a liar, I use your name in vain
But now I'm in some trouble that's kind of hard to explain
And I need your help and I pray that you'll consider
Helpin' me over the borderline
To that beautiful city 'cross the river

I got nothin' to hide 'cause I can't fool you
I've done some things that I shouldn't do
I lost my faith time and time again
Ran from my family and turned my back on my friends
Until my world is just cold, dark and bitter
But I could walk in warm sunshine
In that beautiful city 'cross the river

I never had money, not enough anyway
Never got a break, I struggled day-to-day
And then I met this girl down in Tennessee
And for a few dollars she was real kind to me
But she wanted things that I couldn't give her
But I'll be rich as any king
In that beautiful city 'cross the river

Now I didn't hurt no one, I didn't fire a gun
Just stole what I could and then I began to run
Drove three long days straight to El Paso
With a bag full of cash and visions of Mexico
Now all I'm askin' is that you will deliver
Me over the borderline
To that beautiful city 'cross the river

EVERYBODY LIKES
THE VENTURES, 1981

"So, you don't like The Ventures?" He asked me in a nice but businesslike voice.

I tried not to look at Eddie Nash as I sat in front of his desk. I'd heard the rumors that he was some sort of deadly serious Lebanese gangster who was the major drug supplier to most of southern California. On the other hand, he also owned the club I had just played that night, and he had my band's money that I had come into his office to collect stacked neatly on his desk in front of him. I tried my best to smile and quickly glance at him every now and then.

"No. I like The Ventures," I said looking at the stack of cash. "They're cool, I guess. Always have been. So . . . who says I don't like The Ventures?"

It was my first time in Eddie Nash's inner sanctum office, deep in the bowels of The Starwood nightclub in Hollywood. My band, The Blasters, had just finished our second set of the night and I was still wearing my sweat-drenched stage clothes while my brain was still reeling from more than a little too much beer and loud rock and roll.

"My booking agent told me." His voice was still calm, but he wasn't smiling. "She told me she called you about your band opening up for The Ventures here next month, and you said you weren't interested. Why would you say you weren't interested if, as you say, you like The Ventures?"

At that moment I didn't really know if I liked The Ventures or not, but I knew I liked The Starwood. The Blasters had already played a few shows there and I thought it was everything a rock and roll club should be. The Starwood allowed all ages into shows so kids could drive in from Pomona or Pacoima, get turned on to new cutting-edge bands, and feel like they were an important part of the scene. The Starwood was also dark, smoky, wild, and cavernous with a labyrinth of hallways leading to various rooms, nooks, dead-ends, or mysterious locked doors. Plus, the security guards sometimes looked the other way if you wanted to discretely consume something that could have possibly been illegal.

The Starwood also had a policy of letting in, for free, any musician who'd ever played the club whether you were famous or not, on your way up or on your down. The musicians and scene makers were given full access to the large private balcony to the left of the stage in the main showroom. Once you were up in the balcony, you could watch whatever band was playing from a safe distance, or you could meet and hang out with musicians from every happening (or hoping to be happening) band in town. It didn't matter if you played punk, new wave, R&B, electronic, hard rock, or funk, every musician was welcome on the balcony. You could swap horror stories from bad gigs and bad promoters or try to hustle up an opening slot with whomever was the hot band that month. You could also rub shoulders and flirt with the porn actresses, topless dancers, and escorts who seemed to be permanent fixtures at The Starwood no matter what band was playing.

"I got nothing against The Ventures," I said. "But, um, we've just started headlining your club and we kind, um, feel like we shouldn't be opening for anyone unless it's some band like The Cramps or The Plimsouls or X."

I could feel my confidence starting to slowly build as I spoke. The Blasters had been playing a lot of shows across Southern California, and we were starting to get a good amount of local press, which helped attract bigger and bigger crowds to our shows. We were selling out joints like Club 88, The Hong Kong, and Blackies. We'd even just sold out a show at the Starwood's main competitor, the Whisky a Go Go. I started to feel a bit cocky in Eddie Nash's office because, thanks to our growing popularity, I knew The Starwood wanted us to help fill the club for a show that perhaps wasn't going to do well without an act like us to bring some folks.

"Look, I know what's going on," Eddie Nash said. "You're headlining Tuesdays and Wednesdays. The shows with The Ventures are on a weekend. Weekends are better, don't you think?"

"Yeah. They are better."

"So, then, what's the big problem? Are The Ventures not cool with you?" He snarled a little as he said this. "Do you think you're cooler than

The Ventures? How many number one hits have you had? Tell me. Seriously. How many?"

I had no way of knowing that it was right around this time that Eddie Nash had sent some thugs up to a house in the Hollywood hills to exact bloody vengeance on some lowlifes. Apparently, the lowlifes had somehow broken into Eddie's home, tied him up, and humiliated him physically in various ways before stealing a sizeable quantity of his drugs. Their biggest mistake was leaving Eddie alive, and now he wanted his pride and his drugs back. Four people wound up bludgeoned to death on Wonderland Drive in a brutal killing that Eddie Nash would never be convicted of.

"Well, um, we're still trying to get a record deal," I stuttered. "But please don't get me wrong. The Ventures are alright. They're cool. Everybody likes The Ventures."

"That's right," he shouted. "Everybody likes The Ventures!"

"It's just that, me and the band, well, we've been working really hard, and we think we kind of deserve to headline a weekend on our own—"

"Wait a second!" Eddie Nash raised his hand and cut me off. "You and your guys think what? You want what? Do you and your little band think that playing a fucking weekend at The Starwood with The Ventures is beneath you? Do you think it's something to be embarrassed by? Do you think your cool little fucking friends wouldn't think you were so goddamn cool if you opened for The Ventures? Do you think you're on your way up in this business? Maybe you are. I don't know, and I don't care. All I fucking know is that you're gonna meet me again on your fucking way down."

He paused and stared at me. Then he smiled slightly and said, "Don't get me wrong. I like your band. I like all that old shit you guys play, and your brother has a hell of a voice. I only have one question. Do you and your band ever want to play the fucking Starwood again?"

"Yes, sir. Of course we want to play here again."

"So then what's the big fucking problem?"

"There's no problem, Mr. Nash," I said looking at the stack of money on his desk. "We'd love to play here with The Ventures. They're rock and roll legends."

"Damn right, they're legends. All right. Good. This is good," he said. His voice softened as he smiled sincerely at me. "So, you're gonna play with The Ventures at The Starwood on a weekend. This is good. Good for you. Good for me. I'm very happy we could reach an agreement on this. You do this favor for me, and you won't regret it. I promise it will be good. Everything will be good." As he spoke he slid the stack of money across his desk toward me.

"Thank you, Mr. Nash. It's nice to finally meet you," I said as I stood up, grabbed the money, and backed toward his office door.

"Hey, Blaster, listen," Eddie said, smiling, as I opened the door to leave, "always remember, everybody likes The Ventures."

"Yes, sir. I will. Everybody likes The Ventures."

BLUE BOULEVARD
(A TRIBUTE TO DEL SHANNON AND MY COUSIN DONNA DIXON)
DAVE ALVIN / MICHAEL WOODY

On this empty road in this lonely town
  No one's up when the sun goes down
I turn around and cruise once more
  Past the old park and the abandoned stores
    Oh, baby, it drives me crazy

'Cause every day I work the same old job
  Waiting for the night to fall
Then I'm on this street that once was ours
  Streetlights shining down like stars
    Oh, baby, you drive me crazy
    'Cause I hung your picture around my rearview mirror
But when I look back, you're not there

  And every night I remember
  We took a ride in my car
  I aimed straight for heaven
  But I ended up on Blue Boulevard

Well, it runs as far as I can see
  But that still ain't far enough for me
With the radio on and a full tank of gas
  I'm looking for you on every corner I pass
    Baby, you drive me crazy
    'Cause I can't find you anywhere
    And I spend my whole life going nowhere

And every night I remember
We took a ride in my car
I aimed straight for heaven
But I ended up on Blue Boulevard

I've been chasin' down this white line such a long time

But I end up in the same place but it's the wrong time
And you're not mine,
You just slipped away

And every night I remember
We took a ride in my car
I aimed straight for heaven
But I ended up on Blue Boulevard

DOWNEY TO LUBBOCK
(GEOGRAPHIC AND BIOGRAPHIC DUET)
DAVE ALVIN / JIMMIE DALE GILMORE

DA: Well, I'm a wild blues Blaster from a sunburnt California town
And I've got a loud Stratocaster that can blow any roadhouse down
You know I've been up on the mountain and I've looked for the Promised Land
I've been to the Ash Grove and I shook Lightnin's hand
Now I'm leavin' tonight, people, I'm Downey to Lubbock bound

JDG: Well I'm an old Flatlander from the great high plains
Like wanderlust and wonder, West Texas wind blows through my veins
But it seemed like California was the place to be
For a hippie country singer, that was me
And I'm leavin' tonight, man, I'm Lubbock to Downey bound

DA: Forty years on the highway livin' on dreams and gasoline
And somehow still survivin' on Advil, NyQuil and nicotine
Every city and every heartbreak, every hopeful kiss
Every road that I've traveled has led me to this
Now I'm leavin' tonight, people, I'm Downey to Lubbock bound

JDG: Well, I took a lot of detours, cul-de-sacs and dead ends
But I made a lot of music and I made a lot of friends
I took a lot of turns maybe some were not that good
But if I had to do it over, well I surely mostly would
I'd stay right on this highway that's Lubbock to Downey bound

DA: Well, I'm a wild blues Blaster lookin' to find what can be found

JDG: And I'm an old Flatlander, I've been 'round and 'round and 'round

DA: I know someday this old highway's going to come to an end

JDG: And I know when it does you're gonna be my friend

DA: Now I'm leavin' tonight, people, I'm Downey to Lubbock bound

JDG: Yeah, I'm leavin' tonight, I'm Lubbock to Downey bound

ABILENE
(HOPE SPRINGS ETERNAL BITTER-SWEETLY)

There's a Greyhound bus leavin' the great Northwest
Takin' her tonight back down south to Texas
She's been dancin' on tables
To pay rent and be able
To just get by and maybe stay clean
Abilene, Abilene
Abilene, Abilene

Well, her daddy'd get drunk, then he'd hit her hard
And her momma'd lie in bed, high on pills and talkin' to God
But like her beautiful tattoos
These old memories she can't lose
Since she ran away at fifteen

   Abilene, Abilene, there's a town ahead that
   You've never seen
   And maybe it's better if you
   Get off there and try to
   Forget everything, Abilene

Starin' out the window at the long, cold night
Ahead on the horizon is another string of bright lights
She's dreamin' of a man she's going down to meet
In a bar on an Austin street
And maybe this one won't be so mean

Abilene, Abilene, there's a town ahead that
You've never seen
And maybe it's better if you
Get off there and try to
Forget everything, Abilene

In a Texas bar, there's a man sittin' alone
Thinkin' of a girl he swore he'd wait there for
But he's drinking beers and he's feelin' old
Rememberin' every lie he's told
'Til he changes his mind and he leaves

Abilene, Abilene, there's a town ahead that
You've never seen
And maybe it's better if you
Get off there and try to
Forget everything, Abilene

FOR NANCI GRIFFITH

I just heard Nanci Griffith has moved on to whatever awaits us all on the other side.

Like many of you, I'm in shock and feel terribly sad. Nanci was a very smart, literate songwriter, a uniquely gifted vocalist and a brave, deeply complex artist on par with the best. Though she was a savvy, tough, ambitious person, she was also a generous supporter of young, lesser-known songwriters, as well as a passionate advocate for the innocent victims of landmines and war crimes around the world.

Nanci and I were close for a little while 20 years ago, and in 2001, we shared some intense, heartbreaking, beautiful-yet-painful experiences traveling across Cambodia visiting still-active landmine fields, remote jungle health clinics, struggling hospitals, small silk farms, former killing fields, and even a leper colony. Near the end of our time together there, feeling a touch wild and overconfident, she and I attempted to climb to the top of the tallest temple at Angkor Wat during a heavy rainstorm. Climbing up the high spire on the narrow, wet stone steps was slow and dangerous. I made it, but Nanci fell. Thankfully, besides some gigantic bruises, she wasn't seriously injured. But I remember reaching my hand down to her just before she fell, and how painfully powerless I felt at that moment watching her slip down the spire. I feel the same way now.

I have a photograph I treasure of me and Nanci that was taken in 2000 at a show of mine at the old El Casino Ballroom on the south side of Tucson. She is smiling, cool and confident, her right hand resting on my back, while I'm trying to hide my shyness by glaring sternly at the camera with my left arm draped around her shoulder. My dearest friends, the late Chris Gaffney and the late Bobby Lloyd Hicks (from my band, The Guilty Men), were standing just a few feet away, out of camera range, waiting to go on stage. As I stare now at the photograph, I sincerely wish that I was there with all of them, back on that wonderful night at the El Casino so many years ago.

Rest in peace, Nanci. I'll meet you on the top of the temple.

BUS STATION
(WHERE DREAMS AND LOVE LEAVE TOWN)

Bus station at sun up, lookin' for a new place to go
He sips his Coke, and he pulls his ring and thinks of how she looked years ago
She curls up with a blanket in a yellow plastic seat
He touches her and she looks out the window at an empty morning street
    Well, he must have had a screw loose in his head
    To end up like this after all he's said
    He lies to her, she kisses him
    Gettin' tired of love

Bus station at sun up, she reads the ticket in her hand
It's a different name for the same old town, and this ain't the life that they had planned
So he tries to tell her it won't be like the times before
It's a different town and a brand-new start, and he's gonna work a little bit more
    But he must have had a screw loose in his head
    To end up like this after all he's said
    He lies to her, she kisses him
    Gettin' tired of love

Bus station at sun up, another hour left to blow
He touches her but she'd like to leave
And there's no place left to go
    Well, she must have had a screw loose in her head
    How could she believe all the things he said?
    She lies to him, he kisses her
    Gettin' tired of love
    Gettin' tired of love
    Gettin' tired of love

EVENING BLUES
(ACOUSTIC FINGERPICKING FOLK BLUES)

Standin' barefoot in your kitchen door
Listenin' to the soft evening rain
Watchin' you dryin' off from your shower
   Look at me like you don't know my name

Then you heat the coffee on the stove
   And pull a cup down from the shelf
You slowly turn your back on me
   As I sing a blues song to myself

   Yeah, I wish that I could hold you, baby, but you seem so far away
   Yeah, I wish that I could kiss you, baby, but I've run out of sweet words to say
   And I wish that I could hear, yeah, I wish that I could hear
   The blues you sing to yourself

Now all the makeup is washed off your face
   And your hair is slicked back wet
You hung the dress up you wore last night
   And changed the sheets on your bed

All the promises you whispered to me
   I guess they're meant for someone else
'Cause all I hear is the soft evening rain
   And the blues that I sing to myself

Yeah, I wish that I could hold you, baby, but you seem so far away
Yeah, I wish that I could kiss you, baby, but I've run out of sweet words to say
And I wish that I could hear, oh, I wish that I could hear
The blues you sing to yourself
The blues you sing to yourself

Would you care if I walked out this door?
    Baby, I can't really tell
Our eyes meet but we just look away
    And sing our blues to ourselves

Yeah, I wish that I could hold you, baby, but you seem so far away
Yeah, I wish that I could kiss you, baby, but I've run out of sweet words
    to say
And I wish that I could hear, yeah, I wish that I could hear
The blues you sing
The blues
The blues you sing to yourself

ANYWAY
(FOLK/POP RELATIONSHIP RUMINATIONS)
DAVE ALVIN / AMY FARRIS

Baby, let's get out of this house
I can't stand the mess
I never noticed before
Anyway

Now your silence is just too loud
I'm a stranger and you're a crowd
I think it's time that we
Got away

   Let's drown our sorrows, honey
   And drink up all of our money
   We've said all that there is to say
   Maybe I love you
   Anyway

I didn't mean those words I said
Maybe you didn't either
Or maybe we did
Anyway

Let's just kill another beer
And pretend that we're not here
We'll figure it out
Some other day

   Let's drown our sorrows, honey
   Drink up all of our money
   We've said all that there is to say
   Maybe I love you
   Anyway

BLACK ROSE OF TEXAS
(A COUNTRY BALLAD FOR AMY FARRIS)

All the pills you kept beside your bed
Were never enough to ease your mind
And the men who came but always left
Not all of them treated you real kind
You tried booze and God and cigarettes
But nothing could keep you from cryin'
Black Rose of Texas
I hope you found some peace this time

In the honky tonks and punk rock bars
Sometimes it felt so good to be alive
Doin' the two-step across a hardwood floor
While telling some wild boy white lies
But the music always had to stop
And you had to face the world on your own
Black Rose of Texas
I hope you found your way back home

   Black Rose of Texas
   No one can say you didn't try
   Black Rose of Texas
   I wish I could have said goodbye

On a train in Arizona
As the morning sun was burnin' in the east
A long-distance phone call woke me up from my sleep
Then I watched the desert passing by
Replaying sweet and sad memories
Black Rose of Texas
I hope this time you're finally free

Black Rose of Texas
No one can say you didn't try
Black Rose of Texas
I wish I could have said goodbye
Black Rose of Texas
I hope you found some peace this time
Black Rose of Texas
I just wish I could have said goodbye

ANGEL ON YOUR SHOULDER
(LATE NIGHT COUNTRY REVELATIONS)

You closed down all the barrooms and then drove home at 2 AM
As you told your whole life story to one more drunken man
But he passed out on your sofa so you sit up and watch TV
Changing channel to channel looking for something you've never seen

   Like an angel on your shoulder
   Who'll be with you through the night
   Like an angel on your shoulder
   Who'll make everything all right

You turn a light on in your bedroom and pick up a book you've never read
But the words just run together so you reach for the phone instead
And then you try to remember a number you once know
To tell someone about these good times they're missing not being with you

   There's an angel on your shoulder
   Who'll be with you through the night
   Like an angel on your shoulder
   Who'll make everything all right

Now a cold and grey sunrise cracks the curtains in your room
You toss and turn in your blankets thinking of everything you've been through
Now you're so far from your street days and you still have so far to go
But sometimes you can't believe that you can make it on your own

   There's an angel on your shoulder
   Who'll be with you through the night
   Like an angel on your shoulder
   Who'll make everything all right

There's an angel on your shoulder
Maybe you've never known
That there's an angel on your shoulder
And you'll never be alone
There's an angel on your shoulder
And you'll never be alone

MARIE MARIE
(CALIFORNIA R&B ROCKERS BLAST SWAMPY CAJUN)

Marie Marie
Playin' guitar on the back porch
I sit in my car while you sing so sad
Marie Marie

Marie Marie
It's so lonely in these farmlands
Please come with me to the bright lights downtown
Marie Marie

   I say, hey pretty girl, don't you understand
   I just want to be your lovin' man

Marie Marie
The sun is down in the cornfields
The evening is dark, and you sing so sad
Marie Marie

Marie Marie
I got two weeks in back pay
There's gas in my car and your folks say I must go
Marie Marie

   I say, hey pretty girl, don't you understand
   I just want to be your lovin' man

Marie Marie
Playin' guitar on the back porch
I leave in my car while you sing so sad
Marie Marie

KATHLEEN
(ROCKABILLY GARAGE BAND MEETS
'50S NEW ORLEANS BOOGIE)

Well, I heard on the streets that you're a good girl gone bad
Well, I can't point the finger with the reputation I have
   So tonight, Kathleen, we can be what we want to be
   It's only you and me tonight, Kathleen

Well, I don't want to know where you go with your men
You can tell in my face that I've seen every place you've been
So tonight, Kathleen, we can be what we want to be
   It's only you and me tonight, Kathleen

   And it's don't think twice
   Who can hold it against us now?
   Don't think twice
   We're two different people now, Kathleen

Well, my mom knows yours and they sit together in church
And my dad knows yours and they drink together after work
   So tonight, Kathleen, we can be what we want to be
   It's only you and me tonight, Kathleen

Well, I heard on the streets that you've been in trouble before
Well, I've had my share and I'm gonna have a whole lot more
   So tonight, Kathleen, we can be what we want to be
   It's only you and me tonight, Kathleen

   And it's don't think twice
   Who can hold it against us now?
   Don't think twice
   We're two different people now, Kathleen

MEMPHIS, TENNESSEE, NOVEMBER 1981

There's forty people out there in the audience
In a club that holds three hundred.
I'm backstage in a cement dressing room with a broken mirror
And a nude lightbulb hanging from the ceiling,
Drinking a Budweiser and smoking Kools.

And there's forty people out in the audience
In a club that holds three hundred.
Ten of them are on the guest list.
We have to do three sets
And we're working for the door.
We're minutes from Graceland
Where Elvis died.
We're minutes away from Sun Studios
Where all this rock & roll stuff was born.

The club has posters of '70s rock stars on the walls.
'70s rock stars playing big sports arenas
In front of thousands of fans.
'70s rock stars sweating out their cocaine and limousines
But some guy asks if I'm gonna boogie tonight.
And the club owner says,
"I thought you guys were popular."
And the bar maid says,
"No more free beer."
And people are walking out before the first set.

LONG DISTANCE INFORMATION
GET ME THE FUCK OUT OF MEMPHIS, TENNESSEE!

Back home some people love us.
Back home people hate us that used to love us.
And people hate us that always hated us.
The bank won't cash your press kit
And Nashville wants to cancel.

BOB BIGGS, 1946-2020

I always liked him.
Even when I didn't.

You couldn't help but like the guy.
He was a very charming, visionary rascal.
A smooth, slight shady, sweet jive talker
With a brilliant and perceptive ear for
Musicians, bands, trends, scenes and personalities.
He first documented whatever new group
Tickled his fancy in the pages of his magazine, Slash.
Then, years later, he signed them to his label, Slash Records.

I always liked him but I could bitch
(and I certainly did in my more bitter past)
About various monies owed that were never paid
To many of his bands, visual artists and writers.
At the same time, though, I have to stress
That the wild, cutting edge Los Angeles
Music scene of late '70s / early '80s
Wouldn't have been quite as legendary or wild
Without his unique contributions to it.
And I'll always point out that he gave us Blasters
A chance when no other damn record label would.

Again, I stress he was a brilliant and visionary character,
But when he was wrong he could be incredibly wrong.

My favorite memory of what a seriously odd goofball
He could be was from 1982 when we
Blasters were working on our album, *Non-Fiction.*
He was hanging out every night in the studio,
Usually dragging along a collection of hangers-on
From his Art and Money world into our Blasters world,
Even though we had no idea who they were
Or any interest in most of them.

He cornered me in the studio
Late one night when he was very high.
He conspiratorially whispered to me,
"Let's step outside. I've got a great idea for you."

The two of us stepped out of the studio
And walked a minute down a dark stretch of Sunset Blvd.,
before he stopped me and said,
"I finally figured out what you guys are missing.
It'll make you guys so fucking huge
That you'll blow everyone away, man."

"Wow. Um. Okay. What's the idea?"

I had to take him somewhat seriously
Even if he was jacked up out of his skull.
Not every record label owner back then
Was brave and savvy enough to put out raw records
By The Germs, X, The Blasters, Violent Femmes, Los Lobos,
Rank and File, The Dream Syndicate, Flesh Eaters or The Gun Club.
He was always fully committed that his bands would be
Important, influential and successful in their way.
And they all were.

"I'm shocked I hadn't thought of this before.
It's crazy but hear me out on this."

"Yeah, yeah. So what's your idea?"

He looked at me nervously then proudly declared,
"Trombones! You guys need to add trombones!
Think of it, man . . . The Blasters . . . with trombones!
You've already got the saxes
So the missing magic is trombones!
Everybody gets rich on this idea!"

I nodded, smiled politely,
Promised I'd bring up trombones with the guys,
And, of course, I wisely never did.
Who knows though?
Maybe I should have.

I always liked him,
Even when I didn't.
And even though we hadn't spoken in decades
I'm very sad that's he's not in this world anymore.

GUILTY MAN
(ELECTRIC LATE-NIGHT AMORAL CONFESSIONS)

Well, the guy behind the counter didn't speak good English
  But he understood the point of a gun
It wasn't no big deal, he just had some money
  And at the time I didn't have none
I walked in his store half past midnight
  I took what I could then I ran
So tonight the police are searching this city
  For one more guilty man

Yeah, I think I'll go see this woman on my old side of town
  I like to see her every now and again
And I'll say hi to her kids as she sends them to bed
  'Cause her ex-husband is my best friend
She won't ask no questions, she'll just smile
  When I lay some money in her hands
And for an hour or two she'll say she's in love
  With one more guilty man

  You can blame my folks or the economy
  Blame my schooling or you can blame me
  I'm just what I am, one more guilty man

I could say I got some kids and they got nothin' to eat
   And I got tired of hearin' 'em cry
I could say anything that you wanted to hear
   But it just might be a lie
Yeah, I could get a job, but I got my pride
   I ain't workin' in no hamburger stand
So, take a good look through the bars on your windows
   For one more guilty man

   You can blame my folks or the economy
   Blame my schooling or you can blame me
   I'm just what I am, one more guilty man
   One more guilty man
   Yeah, one more guilty man
   One more guilty man

MARY BROWN
(HOUSING TRACT FOLK NOIR)

My name is Charlie Thomas and I'm as good a man as you
And for the love of Mary Brown there's nothin' that I won't do
Her husband was a banker yet she told me he was cruel
So I left his body lying in the yard where their roses grew

She and I grew up neighbors where the houses look the same
And I swear that I loved Mary Brown before I knew her name
After she married and he moved her away
You know she'd still come back and lay with me like nothin' had ever
changed

   I know what's wrong and right
   What goes around comes around
   But there ain't nothin' that I won't do
   For the love of Mary Brown

Well, people like him always looked down on me
Because I've done a little time for armed robbery
Yeah, but Mary Brown knows I'm from a good family
And she didn't say nothin' when she slipped me the back door key

   I know what's wrong and right
   What goes around comes around
   But there ain't nothin' that I won't do
   For the love of Mary Brown

Well, at my trial she testified she kissed me once or twice
But she swore that was long before she became his wife
And every time I looked at her she avoided my eyes
Then the jury sentenced me to 25 years to life

I haven't seen Mary Brown since the trial's end
And she never answers the letters that I send
And I heard that she married her husband's best friend
Yeah, but for the love of Mary Brown, man, I'd do it all again

   I know what's wrong and right
   What goes around comes around
   But there ain't nothin' that I won't do
   For the love of Mary Brown

MURRIETTA'S HEAD
(A DUSTY HISTORY OF DESPERATE CALIFORNIA)

Come on saddle up, boys, 'cause the governor said
He'll pay three thousand dollars for Murrietta's head

I hear Joaquin Murrietta steals horses and gold
He killed the sheriff in Mariposa, or so I'm told
He's the devil's bloody bastard, wicked and no good
But all the Mexicans swear that he's Robin Hood
Well, with my wife and my sons, I work as hard as I can
On thirteen acres of California land
But the rains never came and I got debts I can't pay
Now the bank's gonna steal my farm away

  Come on saddle up, boys, 'cause the governor said
  He'll pay three thousand dollars for Murrietta's head
  He don't want him alive; he wants him dead
  He'll pay three thousand dollars for Murrietta's head

I hear Joaquin Murrietta rides to avenge
The murder of his wife by a mob of drunk men
But I don't give a damn if it's a lie or if it's true
'Cause for his family, ain't much a man won't do
See the fever came around and my youngest boy took ill
And I didn't have money to pay no doctor's bills
So I buried his body 'neath that oak on the hill
But if I had money, I swear he'd be alive still

Come on saddle up, boys, 'cause the governor said
He'll pay three thousand dollars for Murrietta's head
He don't want him alive; he wants him dead
He'll pay three thousand dollars for Murrietta's head

Well, the Bible says you reap what you sow
Yeah, that could be true, but I really don't know
Well if it is, Murrietta will be damned to hell
And when I kill him I'll be damned as well

Come on saddle up, boys, 'cause the governor said
He'll pay three thousand dollars for Murrietta's head
He don't want him alive; he wants him dead
He'll pay three thousand dollars for Murrietta's head

BILLY THE KID AND GERONIMO
(A FOLK SONG ABOUT A MYTHICAL MEETING)

There's an old story in New Mexico
'Bout the night Billy the Kid met Geronimo
In a Lordsburg barroom, they spoke their minds
One hand on their pistols and cold blood in their eyes

Billy the Kid said to Geronimo
My mother died young and left me all alone
So I grew up wild, my gun my best friend
I killed 21 men and I'd kill them all again

Geronimo said, I've nowhere left to hide
The land of my birth, I don't recognize
There's railroads and barbed wire and towns without end
And my people are scattered like leaves to the wind

Billy the Kid said, We're just the same
We're cursed and we're damned as they whisper our names
We're hunted, we're hated, we're feared and reviled
By every God-fearin' man, woman and child

Geronimo said, No, we're not the same
For the harm that I've done, I feel great shame
But I fought for my family, my tribe and my lands
Yet we'll pay the same price for the blood on our hands

As the morning sun rose and the coyotes cried
The Chiricahua and the outlaw said goodbye
And rode across the desert their separate ways
One prison bound and the other to his young grave
One prison bound and the other to his young grave

ANDERSONVILLE
(FOLK BALLAD FOR ASA POWELL)

In the spring of '61 I kissed my mother goodbye
I put on a blue uniform and I fought for Lincoln's side
Until I got caught by Johnny Reb in the woods near Chapel Hill
I wish to God he had killed me there but he sent me to Andersonville

My uniform is faded and there's no boots on my feet
And I'm pullin' worms out of the mud 'cause there's nothin' else to eat
And the rebs can't even feed their own so there's no way they can fill
The bellies of us Yankees starving in Andersonville

Some men are born to preach God's word
And some men are born to kill
And I guess that I was only born to die in Andersonville

I dug a hole with my bare hands in the red Georgia clay
'Cause there ain't no shelter from the sun or the cold winds or the rain
And I'm too damn weak to stand up at all so I just lay quiet and still
And they can bury me in the hole I dug when I die in Andersonville

I dream the same dream every night of a woman I've never known
She's standin' by a warm fireside and she whispers that I've come home
And in the morning when I wake I pray someday that she'll
Lay a flower on my grave when I die in Andersonville

Some men are born to preach God's word
And some men are born to kill
And I guess that I was only born to die in Andersonville
Lord, I guess that I was only born to die in Andersonville

PUBLIC DOMAIN
LINER NOTES

Old folk songs are spirits.

They live in the silence of the mountains and deserts,
They live in the thick mud along our rivers,
In the dirt beneath endless miles of tract homes and shopping malls,
In the darkness beyond the bright lights
   of interstate highways, truck stops and office towers,
In abandoned buildings, closed factories, deserted farms,
   lost battlefields, forgotten graveyards, empty prairies,
   in blues bars, honky tonks, railyards, barnyards,
   backyards, church choirs and bedrooms.

Like ancient redwoods and giant seqouias,
Our folk songs endure beyond
   (and in spite of)
The whims of current popular taste
And the quick gratifications of our disposable culture.

Our folk songs live in the wild lands of our hearts.

They aren't relics from an idealized, sentimental past.

Our folk songs are about love,
Jealousy, anger, longing, revenge, despair, survival and hope for the future.
They're hard, sad, rowdy,
Tender and joyous images of who we were,
Where we come from,
Who we are, where we're headed

And who we could become.
A lot of what is good about us
And bad about us
Is in these songs.

They are in the Public Domain.
They belong to nobody.
They belong to all of us.

DRY RIVER
(FINDING HOPE AND STRENGTH
IN AN UNLIKELY PLACE)

I was born by a river
But it was paved with cement
I was born by a river
But it was paved with cement
Still I'd stand in that dry river
And dream that I was soaking wet

   Someday it's gonna rain
   Someday it's gonna pour
   Someday that old dry river
   Lord, it won't be dry anymore

I played in the orange groves
'Til they bulldozed all the trees
I played in the orange groves
Until they bulldozed all the trees
Still, I'd stand among the dead stumps
And smell the blossoms on the leaves

   Someday it's gonna rain
   Someday it's gonna pour
   Someday all those dead trees
   Lord, they won't be dead any more

I fell in love with a woman
But she did not fall for me
I fell in love with you, baby,
Oh, but you did not fall for me
Now, I'm as dry as that old river
And I'm as dead as those old trees

   Someday it's gonna rain
   Someday it's gonna pour
   Someday this old heart of mine's
   Gonna fall in love once more

   Someday it's gonna rain
   Someday it's gonna pour
   Someday that old dry river
   Lord, it won't be dry any more

FAR AWAY
(MEMORIES OF A BOY'S SUMMER EVENINGS)

On a summer night a boy rides his bike
Away from a sundown city
He's headed for a trail and a dry riverbed
He's going far, far away

Past old trees and dead factories
The wind howlin' in his ears
Then through a gate that no one locked
He's going far, far away

  He's going far, far away
  A new star is starting to rise
  The evening wind brings a tear to his eyes
  He's going far, far away

His mother is worried, stares out the window
And his father don't say a word
As she dreams of a boy she held in her arms
Who's going far, far away

And a stray dog barks, chases his bike
And he can't hear his mother's call
'Cause he's racing a train headin' straight for the night
He's going far, far away

  He's going far, far away
  A new star is starting to rise
  The evening wind brings a tear to his eyes
  He's going far, far away
  So far, far away

Soon Indians ride right by his side
And a cavalry bugle blows
And mountains rise from his hometown streets
Far away
Far away
So far, far away
Far, far away
Far, far away
Far, far away

EVERETT RUESS
(THE MYSTERY OF A YOUNG POET)

I was born Everett Ruess, I've been dead for 60 years
I was just a young boy in my twenties, the day I disappeared
Into the Grand Escalante badlands, near the Utah/Arizona line
And they never found my body, boys, or understood my mind

I grew up in California, and I loved my family and my home
But I ran away to the High Sierras, where I could live free and alone
Folks said, "He's just another wild kid, and he'll grow out of it in time"
But they never found my body, boys, or understood my mind

I broke broncos with the cowboys, sang healing songs with the Navajo
I did the snake dance with the Hopi and I drew pictures everywhere I'd go
And I swapped all my drawings for provisions, to get what I needed to get by
And they never found my body, boys, or understood my mind

But I hate your crowded cities, full of sad and hopeless mobs
And I hate your grand cathedrals, where you try to trap God
'Cause I know God is here in the canyons with the rattlesnakes and pinion pines
And they never found my body, boys, or understood my mind

They say I was killed by a drifter, or I froze to death in the snow
Maybe mauled by a wildcat or I'm livin' down in Mexico
But my end, it doesn't really matter, all that counts is how you live your life
And they never found my body, boys, or understood my mind

Because you give your dreams away as you get older, oh but I never gave
up mine
And they'll never find my body, boys, or understand my mind

MANZANITA
(DEDICATED TO FOLKSINGERS
JIM RINGER AND MARY MCCASLIN)
DAVE ALVIN / CHRISTY MCWILSON

(both DA and CMcW):
Manzanita growin' wild on the hillsides
Where sage and eucalyptus fill the air
Through the years I've dreamed of returning
But in my heart the Manzanita's there

DA:
Her parents never liked it when I took her
Walkin' in the canyons after sundown
Through the cactus and sage and Manzanita
'Til we found a secret place to lay down

CMcW:
In the wintertime the rain beats on my window
And in spring I watch the cherry blossoms grow
So far from my youth in California
So far from a boy I used to know

Manzanita growin' wild on the hillsides
Where sage and eucalyptus fill the air
Through the years I've dreamed of returning
But in my heart the Manzanita's there

CMcW:
Now I see my daughter's face in the mirror
And I wonder if she'll do what I had done
And walk with her love through the canyons
Then leave his arms, turn away and run

149

DA:
They built houses and highways near the hillsides
And I've married and divorced twice since then
But there's still Manzanita in the canyons
Where I pray someday I'll walk with her again

Manzanita growin' wild on the hillsides
Where sage and eucalyptus fill the air
Through the years I've dreamed of returning
But in my heart the Manzanita's there
Through the years I've dreamed of returning

THE DAY AFTER SEEING JIMI HENDRIX WHEN I WAS 13 YEARS OLD

After hiking for over three hours in the San Gabriel Mountains,
The three old men decided to rest next to a small creek
In the shade of a few ancient oak trees.

I sat a short distance from my old man, Jack, and Tex
As we ate sandwiches, potato chips, dried fruits, and Vienna sausages.

I drank water from my canteen
While my old man took a couple sips from a small flask of vodka
Before he passed it to the other old men,
They discussed sports, news they heard on TV,
The wars they'd survived (World War II and Korea),
And criticized the current one in Vietnam.

I was thankful they decided to take a break
Because I hadn't slept the night before
And my body was starting to quit on me.

My old man had gotten me out of bed at 5 AM
For the drive to the mountains
By singing an old Polish song he'd learned as a child
And I didn't want to disappoint him
By skipping a rare hike together
But all I wanted to do was think of Jimi Hendrix.

The evening before the hike, my mother had driven
My pals Joe Cencak, Greg Trousdale, and me
To the Fabulous Forum to see Jimi Hendrix play live.

She warned us not to drink or eat anything inside,
Not to talk to anyone who wasn't a policeman
Or Forum employee or it's medical staff,
Then she waited patiently outside in the parking lot
While inside Jimi Hendrix played as a small riot occurred.

My old man lit a Tareyton cigarette after lunch
As Jack rolled his own from a tobacco pouch and Tex lit up his pipe.

I sat daydreaming, half asleep, staring at the wilderness
Of granite boulders, oaks, pines and manzanitas,
While still hearing Jimi Hendrix
Channeling the blues from outer space
And picturing the gorgeous hippie women
Dancing in the aisles as police and security guards
Tried in vain to get them to sit down.

"David, don't move," my old man growled quietly yet sternly.

"Don't worry. It'll pass by," Jack said calmly.

Tex smiled and pointed with his pipe, "By your left foot, boy."

I looked down at a rattlesnake slowly passing next to my hiking boot.

I closed my eyes and opened them again repeatedly
As I felt my head heating up and my feet starting to freeze in fear.

But then I recalled my old man softly singing the old Polish song
While at the same time I still heard Jimi Hendrix
Conjuring up distorted, magnificent, unpredictable sounds
From his guitar that no one had done before or ever would again.

I felt my fear slowly slipping away
As I focused on the music blasting in my brain
Even though the rattlesnake would stop
Again and again for several seconds by my foot
Before inching its way slowly towards the creek.

I kept listening to this strange but comforting musical mix
Of my old man's tender old Polish song
And Jimi Hendrix's new, brave American one
Until the snake disappeared safely into the bushes.

I didn't know whether it was the time or the snake or the vodka,
But the old men decided to turn around after lunch
And head back down the mountains.

As we hiked,
I thought about the dangerous yet inspiring beauty of nature.
I thought about my old man and his sweet song
I thought about the uncontrollable power of Jimi Hendrix
And I thought about how maybe music,
Whether it was old or new or both,
Could get me through whatever rough situations
My life may have waiting down the trail for me.

NANA AND JIMI
(PSYCHEDELIC FOLK STRUT)

My mother told me to be a good boy
   And don't do nothin' wrong
Then she wrapped up a sandwich
   For me to take along
'Cause I was going to see Jimi
   And nothing's gonna be the same

She drove us crosstown in her old Chevy
   She parked and waited for us outside
She said, "Be careful, honey,
   Of those crazy people inside"
'Cause I was going to see Jimi
   And nothing's gonna be the same

Now there were police at the front door
   And there were police on the stage
But to a twelve-year-old boy
   It was all cool and strange
'Cause I was going to see Jimi
   And nothing's gonna be the same

The lights were dimming, people were shoutin'
   And I forgot about my mom in her car
When he walked out onstage
   And plugged in his guitar
'Cause I was going to see Jimi
   And nothing's gonna be the same
'Cause I was going to see Jimi
   And nothing's gonna be the same

RED ROSE
(METHAMPHETAMINE ROCKABILLY LOVE SONG)

Your father sat with the night's first drink
Your mother washed the dishes in the sink
And you stood on the steps, wearing your best,
One red rose on a new black dress

Well, we walked under the power lines
And I'd dreamed about it a thousand times
You weren't like the rest
One red rose on a new black dress

   One Red Rose on a new black dress
   Crushing it between our chests
   But tonight, I wonder where you'll be
   One dead rose is all I see

Well, we hid in the weeds and we hid in the grass
Listening to the cars on the highway pass
Then you put me to the test
One red rose on a new black dress

   One Red Rose on a new black dress
   Crushing it between our chests
   Tonight, I wonder where you'll be
   One dead rose is all I see

Well, you said we could never go back
Walked away through the housing tract
Leavin' me with what's left
One red rose from a new black dress

Well it's one Red Rose on a new black dress
Crushing it between our chests
And tonight, I wonder where you'll be
One dead rose is all I see

DOWNEY GIRL
(FOR KAREN CARPENTER)

There was once a young girl who lived in my hometown
And she became famous the whole world 'round
With the voice of an angel, singing sweet suburban songs
But no one in our hometown knew anything was wrong
'Cause she was a Downey girl
She was a Downey girl

Well, I never liked her music, I never saw her hangin' around
And I never said nothin' when people put her down
But now that I'm older I can understand her pain
And I can feel a little pride when people say her name
'Cause she was a Downey girl
She was a Downey girl

Tonight I'm on a highway, a thousand years from my hometown
Missin' friends and family who are no longer around
Then I hear her singing on the car radio
A sweet suburban song from a long time ago
And I think about her sadness and I think about her pain
And for a few sweet minutes I'm back home again
'Cause she was a Downey girl
She was a Downey girl

BLACK HAIRED GIRL
(LATE NIGHT URBAN BLUES PONDERINGS)

There's a black-haired girl sittin' behind bulletproof glass
And she takes my money before I go and pump some gas
There's a cold rain falls on the parking lot, the strip malls and housing tracts
I smile at her but she don't smile back

Well, the black-haired girl is starin' at her gossip magazine
At all the glossy pictures of today's kings and queens
Well, it's nearly 3 AM and the whole world is dead except for her and me
And the sound of the rain and the smell of gasoline

Well, that black-haired girl looks like a woman I used to know
Back in some other world several lifetimes ago
Yeah, we'd lay in her bed drinkin' wine and makin' love and lettin' time
    move slow
Well, we lost touch somehow but that's just the way things go

Well, that black-haired girl catches me lookin' her way
And I feel a little uneasy, maybe there's something I should say
Should I ask her name
Or just warn her about all the tricks time can play
But I don't say nothin' 'cause she's gonna find out anyway

There's a black-haired girl sittin' beneath a fluorescent light
And whatever fate has in store, well I hope that she'll be alright
I hope she finds real love
And all her dreams come true or, at least, she makes it through tonight
Then I drive away and she fades out of sight

EVERY NIGHT
ABOUT THIS TIME
(COUNTRY BALLAD FOR GEORGE JONES)

Every night about this time
She's waitin' for a man
It could be me, it could be you
Who'll touch her with their hands
'Cause someone left her long ago
And she never found out why
So she falls in love again
Every night about this time

Every night about this time
She'll be holdin' someone tight
Faces don't mean much
When she turns out her lights
So just tell her that you love her
Even though she knows you're lyin'
And she'll lead you to her room
Every night about this time

Every night about this time
She could be yours, and she could be mine
Just hold her when she cries
Every night about this time

And every night about this time
She'll pretend the best she can
It could be me, it could be you
Who'll remind her of a man

So don't say a word when you leave
There's no need for long goodbyes
'Cause you're not the one she's missin'
Every night about this time

    Every night about this time
    She could be yours, and she could be mine
    So just hold her when she cries
    Every night about this time
    Just hold her when she cries
    Every night about this time
    Just hold her when she cries
    Every night about this time

BORDER RADIO
(TRUE LOVE KNOWS NO BOUNDARIES)

It's one more midnight and her man is still gone
The night moves too slow
She tries to remember the heat of his touch
While listening to the border radio

She calls toll free and requests an old song
Somethin' they used to know
And she prays to herself that wherever he is
He's listening to the border radio

  This song comes from 1962
  Dedicated to a man who's gone
  50,000 watts out of Mexico
  This is the border radio
  This is the border radio

She thinks of her son asleep in his room
And how her man won't see him grow
She thinks of her life and she hopes for a change
While listenin' to the border radio

  This song comes from 1962
  Dedicated to a man who's gone
  50,000 watts out of Mexico
  This is the border radio
  This is the border radio

They play her tune but she can't concentrate
She's wondering why he had to go
It's one more midnight and her man is still gone
And she's listenin' to the border radio

   This song comes from 1962
   Dedicated to a man who's gone
   50,000 watts out of Mexico
   This is the border radio
   This is the border radio
   This is the border radio

FROM A KITCHEN TABLE
(HOMETOWN FOLK SONG FOR AN OLD FRIEND)

I hope this letter finds you,
Wherever you may be
'Cause I mailed some a while back
But they were all returned to me
There ain't nothin' I can tell you 'bout the hometown
Everything changes but nothing's new
Just Sunday night at the kitchen table
Finishin' a beer and thinkin' of you

    And I still work the same job,
    Still live with my mom for free
    Ever since the old man passed on
    It just got harder to leave

I heard a rumor that you got married
Though you swore that you never would
I guess you finally got your own kids now
Do you ever tell 'em 'bout the old neighborhood?
Like the time we stole your dad's car
Drove all night down Imperial Highway
You kept sayin', "Maybe we should turn 'round"
And I said, "It don't take much to get away"

    But I still work the same job
    Still live with my mom for free
    And ever since the old man passed on
    It just got harder to leave

I guess that's all that I got to tell you
Guess things turned out how they're meant to be
I just hope that this letter finds you
But until then, I'll just keep it with me

    And I still work the same job
    Still live with my mom for free
    And ever since the old man passed on
    It just got harder to leave

WEST OF THE WEST
LINER NOTES
JANUARY 2006

One afternoon in 1969, my mother and I were eating lunch at the kitchen table and watching a local LA daytime talk show on our black-and-white TV. The host introduced a young singer/songwriter named John Stewart. He sang "Daydream Believer," a song he wrote that The Monkees had covered and made into a massive hit. I'd always kind of liked the song, but, in my infinite 13-year-old wisdom, I thought The Monkees were pretty jive so I didn't really listen closely. But then he did "July, You're a Woman," and he sang the line, "I have not been known as the Saint of San Joaquin." My mother smiled and said, "He's singing about where I'm from, the San Joaquin Valley." Then I paid closer attention. The TV host asked Stewart questions about songwriting, his time in The Kingston Trio, and about growing up in California. I don't remember his answers, but when he sang "California Bloodlines" at the end of the show, I do remember my mother telling me, "That's what you have, just like him, you've got California bloodlines." Maybe that was when the idea for this CD first entered my mind.

While California doesn't quite have the deep, indigenous folk music traditions of Mississippi, Texas, or Georgia, it does boast a rich history of jazz, blues, R&B, country, and early rock and roll. California has also produced more than its share of damn good songwriters. So, who is and who isn't a California songwriter? It's hard to say. Woody Guthrie lived in California for a few years and wrote many of his signature songs during that period. Union activist/martyr Joe Hill, blues poet laureate Percy Mayfield, and country standard powerhouse Harlan Howard all came out to California and wrote some of their most important songs here. Sam Cooke, Neil Young, Leiber and Stoller, Richard Thompson, Willie Dixon, Gram Parsons, Joni Mitchell, Warren Zevon, Leonard Cohen,

Los Tigres del Norte, and Bob Dylan all made this state their adoptive home. Buck Owens and Wynn Stewart weren't born in California, but they arrived here and helped create the Bakersfield / West Coast country sound. Jesse Belvin, Johnny Guitar Watson, or Sly Stone weren't born in California either, but they did grow up here, and their approaches to blues and soul defined West Coast R&B. Some great California songs weren't written by natives, for example: "California Blues" by Jimmie Rodgers or Guthrie's "Do-Re-Mi," "California Earthquake" by Lightnin' Hopkins or "LA Freeway" by Guy Clark, Terry Allen's "There Ought to be a Law Against Sunny Southern California" or "Los Angeles" by Exene Cervenka and John Doe from X? I guess they could all be considered California songwriters in some way or another.

As I considered what songwriters to choose for this CD, though, I first tried to limit the choices to only people born in California. John Stewart was born in San Diego. Merle Haggard in Bakersfield. Tom Waits in Pomona. Brian Wilson in Hawthorne. Tom Russell in Inglewood. David Hidalgo and Louie Perez in Los Angeles. Kate Wolf, "Blackie" Farrell, Jerry Garcia, and John Fogerty were all born in the greater San Francisco Bay area. Then, unfortunately, I discovered that three major California songwriters weren't born in the state. Fresno's Jim Ringer was born in Arkansas, Fullerton's Jackson Browne was born in Germany, and LA R&B legend Richard Berry was born in Louisiana. Since all three came to California as children, and grew up here, I came up with a loose guideline of "Well, if they weren't born in California, they at least had to have had their first kiss or broken heart out here." I believe all the songwriters I've chosen were shaped, in one way or another, by California's mix of cultures, beliefs, and attitudes, as well as by the oaks and redwoods, the cities and farmlands, the highways and barrooms, the ocean, mountains and deserts, and the eternal hopes and disappointments of growing up in a mythical promised land.

I also tried to limit my choices to songwriters who came, more or less, out of the "roots" tradition of folk, blues, R&B, and country because that's where I come from (and because the huge amount of songs written out here for the commercial pop music/movie/TV industries—not to mention the jazz scene—would be an overwhelming task). Most of these writers helped me define myself as a songwriter and as a Californian. I first heard their songs on jukeboxes and Top 40 AM radio when I was a kid—or on folk and underground music FM radio shows when I was a teenager—while others I heard sung live in smoky bars and honky tonks. I never met some of the writers, while I've been blessed to have crossed paths with others (I once shared a dressing room with Richard Berry and was too intimidated being in the same room with the man who wrote "Louie Louie" to say one word to him). And I've been fortunate enough to have cowritten songs with others.

Over the years the landscapes that shaped these songwriters have vanished or changed drastically. Some of the musical/social worlds that nurtured them have come and gone. Small towns are now big cities that sprawl beyond the horizon, submerging many of the citrus groves, cattle ranches, and oak studded hillsides under layers of freeways, tract homes, shoe box apartments, billionaire mansions, mini-malls, mega-malls, industrial parks, self-storage compounds, doughnut shops, video stores, and nail salons. Musical styles have changed with the landscapes and population, but the tradition continues. Children of Cambodian immigrants compose hip-hop verses on the streets of Long Beach, while young Mexican immigrants sing narco-corridos in the barrooms of Stockton. Right now—whether on a cattle ranch near Alturas, or in an Orange County tract house garage, or in a shack in the woods above Mendocino, or in a one-room apartment in Hollywood—somebody is writing the next generation of songs with California bloodlines.

KING OF CALIFORNIA
(GOLDEN STATE FOLK SONG FOR MY MOTHER)

Well, I left my home and my one true love
　　East of the Ohio River
Her father said we'd never wed
　　For I had neither gold nor silver
But my darling dear, please shed no tears
　　For I think that it's fair to warn ya
That I'll return to claim your hand
　　As the King of California

Over deserts hot and mountains cold
　　I traveled the Indian country
Whisperin' your name under lonesome skies
　　And your memory my only company
But my darling dear, please have no fears
　　For I think that it's fair to warn ya
That I'll return to claim your hand
　　As the King of California

I went up from Sacramento town
　　To the Sierra goldfields
And I worked my stake on a riverbank
　　Dreaming just how a rich man feels
Now my darling dear, listen here
　　For I think that it's fair to warn ya
That I'll return to claim your hand
　　As the King of California

Now, a dead man's lying at my feet
He tried to steal my earnings
Yet I still recall your tender kiss
   Though his bullet in my chest is burnin'
Oh my darling dear, please shed no tears
   'Cause I think that it's fair to warn ya
That I'll return to claim your hand
   As the King of California
That I'll return to claim your hand
   As the King of California

CALIFORNIA'S BURNING
(OMINOUS MENACING BLUES)

California's burning, you can smell it in the air
California's burning, you can smell it in the air
You may be rich or poor but you know that fire don't care

Coyotes howling, devil winds are startin' to blow
Coyotes howling, the devil wind is startin' to blow
And them fires gettin' closer than they were one hour ago

No rain for four years, and the hills are dry and brown
Yeah, no rain for four years, and the hills are dry and brown
Yeah, well, where you gonna run to when the whole wide world burns
 down?

California's burning, there's trouble in the promised land
California's burning, there's trouble in the promised land
You better pack up your family, and you better get out while you can

Now red flames are growin' at the top of the hill
See them red flames growin' at the top of the hill
Well, if the fire don't get you, well, you know the mudslide will

Black clouds are rising and they're blockin' out the sun
Black clouds are rising and they're blockin' out the sun
Some folks are sayin' that Judgement Day has come

California's burning, no one knows when it will end
California's burning, no one knows when this will end
Well, what the fire burns down, boys, we'll just build it back again

CALIFORNIA SNOW
(VERY SLOW FOLK BALLAD)
DAVE ALVIN / TOM RUSSELL

I'm just tryin' to make a living, I'm an old man at thirty-nine
With two kids and an ex-wife who moved up to Riverside
I'm workin' down on the border, drivin' back roads every night
In the mountains east of El Cajon, north of the Tecate line
   Where the California summer sun can burn right to your soul
   In the winter, you can freeze to death in the California snow

I catch the ones I'm able to and watch the others slip away
I know some by their faces and I even know some by name
I guess they think that we're all movie stars and millionaires
I guess that they still believe dreams come true up here
   But I bet the weather's warmer down in Mexico
   And no one ever tells them 'bout the California snow

Last winter I found a man and wife just about daybreak
Layin' in a frozen ditch just south of the Interstate
I wrapped 'em both in blankets, but she'd already died
The next day we sent him back alone across the borderline
   I don't know where they came from or where they planned to go
   But he carried her all night long through the California snow

Some nights when I'm alone out here, I get to thinkin' about my life
Maybe I should go to Riverside and try to fix things with my wife
Or maybe just get in my truck and drive as far as I can go
Away from all the ghosts that haunt the California snow
   Where the California summer sun can burn right to your soul
   But in the winter you can freeze to death in the California snow
   In the winter you can freeze to death in the California snow

OUT IN CALIFORNIA
(LOOKING OUT A BAR WINDOW IN TROMSO, NORWAY)
DAVE ALVIN / TOM RUSSELL

Well, I'm sittin' here drinkin' in the last bar on Earth
Yeah, I'm sittin' here drinkin' in the last bar on Earth
And she's out in California takin' off her tight red skirt

Well the mountains 'round here look just like a woman lying naked on her bed
Yeah, the mountains 'round here look just a woman lying naked on her bed
Well she's out in California but I can't get her out of my head
Out in California

Well they killed all the Indians and they shot all the grizzly bears
Yeah, out in California they killed every grizzly bear
But she's just standing by the window combin' out her long black hair

If a man keeps runnin' he's gonna run right into himself
If a man keeps on movin' he'll run right into himself
But she's out in California laying down with somebody else
Out in California
Out in California

Well I may buy me a Chevy soon as my luck turns around
Or I may buy me a Ford soon as my luck turns around
And then I'm gonna drive right back to that California town

Well, I'm sittin' here drinkin' in the last bar on Earth
Yeah, I'm sittin' here drinkin' in the last bar on Earth
And she's out in California takin' off her tight red skirt

Out in California
Out in California
Out in California

HALEY'S COMET
(ROCK AND ROLL PIONEER LOST IN A BORDER TOWN)
DAVE ALVIN / TOM RUSSELL

"Do you know who I am?" said Bill Hayley
In a pancake house near the Rio Grande
Well the waitress said, "I don't know you from diddley
To me, you're just another tired old man"

Well, he walked all alone down on Main Street
A hot wind was blowin' up from the south
There were two eyes starin' in a pawn shop window
And a whiskey bottle was lifted up to his mouth

There was no moon shinin' on the Rio Grande
As a truck of migrants drove through town
And the jukebox was busted at the bus depot
When Hayley's comet hit the ground

Well he blacked out all the windows in his bedroom
And he was talkin' to the ceilings and the walls
And he closed his eyes, and hit the stage in 1955
As the screams of the children filled the hall

There was no moon shinin' on the Rio Grande
As a truck of migrants drove through town
And the jukebox was busted at the bus depot
When Hayley's comet hit the ground

Well this cop walks into a pancake house in Texas
And he ordered up a couple of cups to go
Then he tells the waitress, "Hey, I just found the body
Of some guy who was famous long ago"

   There was no moon shinin' on the Rio Grande
   As a truck of migrants drove through town
   And the jukebox was busted at the bus depot
   When Hayley's comet hit the ground

BETWEEN THE CRACKS
(A DUSTY HOPEFUL PRAYER)
DAVE ALVIN / TOM RUSSELL

Sundown on the San Joaquin, and an old woman walks home from work
From another day in the fields, another day in the dirt
She lights a sacred candle next to an old photograph
And says a prayer for a boy who fell between the cracks

She stares at a photo of this young boy who caused so much pain
In countless 12-round bloodbaths when Kid Jesus was his name
And he was the pride of the Valley 'til the night he stayed down on his back
And when he took the dive he disappeared down between the cracks

   She says "Jesus was born a poor boy on the wrong side of the tracks
   And he rose again but not before he fell between the cracks"

She rereads the one letter that he wrote her from down in LA
And he said, "Please don't worry 'bout me 'cause I'll come back again someday."
But she remembers every story that's whispered behind her back
About a shooting outside a liquor store somewhere between the cracks

   She says "Jesus was born a poor boy on the wrong side of the tracks
   And he rose again but not before he fell between the cracks"

Sunrise on the San Joaquin and an old woman walks off to work
To another day in the fields, another day in the dirt
She looks around at the children dropping rich men's fruit in their sacks
And she says a prayer for all of us trapped between the cracks

   She says "Jesus was born a poor boy on the wrong side of the tracks
   And he rose again but not before he fell between the cracks
   And he rose again but not before he fell between the cracks"

175

RIO GRANDE
(LOVE IS AS LONG AS A RIVER)
DAVE ALVIN / TOM RUSSELL

I guess she put her blue dress on and walked out late last night
Left one silk stocking dangling from the bedside light
I sobered up and called her name just before the dawn
Saw her boot prints in the sand and knew that she had gone
Down the Rio Grande

I pulled out of Albuquerque prayin' I wasn't late
I got a couple cups of coffee at some joint off the Interstate
Passin' through Las Cruces I swear I saw her car
She always said she'd go someday but never said how far
Down the Rio Grande

Maybe she's in Brownsville, she's got some family there
She was always talkin' 'bout the salty Gulf Coast air
Where the river ends down the Rio Grande

I saw an old grey heron flying south against the wind
And storm clouds over Juarez rolling east to the Big Bend
I drove down Highway 90 through a dusty desert rain
I didn't know where it would lead me or if I'd find her again
Down the Rio Grande

I lit my last cigarette as the sky began to clear
Black mountains up ahead, a red sundown in my mirror
Lost on the border 'tween the future and the past
One fading slowly and the other comin' fast

Maybe she's in Brownsville, she's got some family there
She was always talkin' 'bout the salty Gulf Coast air
Where the river ends down the Rio Grande

I bought a bottle in Del Rio and I parked off the side of the road
I stayed up all night starin' at the lights of Mexico
Then I walked down to the border bridge at the break of day
And I threw that empty bottle off and watched it float away
Down the Rio Grande

Maybe she's in Brownsville, she's got some family there
She was always talkin' 'bout the salty Gulf Coast air
Where the river ends down the Rio Grande
Where the river ends

MOSES ON MOUNT SINAI—
ONE NIGHT IN ITALY
LINER NOTES FOR REISSUE OF
TERRY ALLEN'S *JUAREZ*

A few years ago in Italy, I watched Terry Allen pull an electric piano off its stand, raise it above his head like an angry Moses on Mount Sinai, then violently throw the helpless instrument to the stage with such righteous fury that the piano shattered into a hundred useless pieces. He stood calmly above the wreckage, grinning proudly.

Why he did it, I don't know, but I have to admit that I was more than a little scared. I was standing just a few feet from him, performing a Bo Diddley song in one of those end-of-the-show jam session/singalongs with Terry, Guy Clark, Butch Hancock, Peter Case, Tom Russell, and the Austin band Loose Diamonds when he decided to murder the piano. What scared me wasn't seeing someone destroy a musical instrument—I'd seen plenty of that over the years—but the look in Terry's eyes. These weren't the eyes of Terry Allen, world renowned sculptor, legendary songwriter, and Texas visionary, but the cold eyes of Jabo, the homesick killer pachuco from *Juarez*.

Juarez, Terry Allen's first masterpiece, is one of the great "songwriter" records. Originally recorded and released in the mid-1970s, it stands equal with mandatory seventies songwriter classics like Dylan's *Blood on the Tracks* and Randy Newman's *Good Old Boys*, and it stands equal (or above) any made in the decades since. Like Dylan's and Newman's songs, the songs on *Juarez* work on so many levels that they defy easy categorization or neat explanations. Like old anonymous folk ballads, the narrative songs on *Juarez* tell one story, but inside the seemingly simple story is a universe of other stories, myths, lovers, barrooms, highways, dead ends, and meanings. You can appreciate each song on the level of "That's a good song" or "That's a good drinking song." Or you can, if you're so disposed, delve into their deeper meanings. Is *Juarez* a commentary on the history of the wild west, the conquest and colonization of the Americas, the alienation and dislocation of modern American life, or all of the above? Or none?

There are many songs on *Juarez* that are as scary as that crashing piano. "There Ought to be a Law Against Sunny Southern California" is one of the baddest bad-boy ballads to come out of the still-wild west. But there are also bittersweet moments of honky-tonk existentialism—"La Despe-dida" still stuns me with its sad beauty every time I hear it—as well as transcendental humor like "Writing On Rocks Across The U.S.A." There are even songs that mix humor and violence with touching innocence and desperate passion. Not an easy task. Just ask any poet or songwriter.

Another reason *Juarez* was so powerful when it was first recorded—and is still just as intense today—is the simplicity and intimacy of the recording. With only his words and piano (plus some subtle yet excellent guitar and mandolin accompaniment), Terry Allen manages to paint the border town whorehouses, the small mountain town trailer park, and the dark desert highways with all the vivid colors of a Maynard Dixon painting. The sparseness of the tracks allows his voice to inhabit every character with a credibility that might have been lessened with more elaborate arrangements. Like Hank Williams or Robert Johnson, Terry Allen is capable of making you believe every word he sings. The anger, disappointment, lust, loneliness, love, hope, and hopelessness of Jabo, Chic, Spanish Alice, and Sailor come to life in Allen's "I've been there and back" vocals. As I saw in his eyes as he killed the piano on stage, you would swear the *Juarez* characters possess him as much as he possesses them.

Juarez is that intense of a work of art (or poetry or music or whatever you want to call it) by a master, if sadly underrated, songwriter. A work of art that tells a story with no end, with maybe no noble heroes and possibly no uplifting moral lesson to be learned but, nonetheless, it's a story that had to be told. Just like that piano had to be destroyed one night in Italy.

DEATH OF THE LAST STRIPPER
(A EULOGY FOR A SMALLTOWN GIRL)
DAVE ALVIN / TERRY ALLEN / JO HARVEY ALLEN

She had a boy with some guy from Fresno
But where he is now, none of us know
We found a number on a paper in her purse
That was the number that we called first

Oh, but nobody answered
Every time that we tried
We're the only ones in the world
Who even knew that she died

Gave her clothes to the Goodwill except for one pretty dress
Did her hair and her makeup so she'd look her best
Got carnations at the Safeway, there were no roses there
Had no money for a preacher so we just said a prayer

Oh, but nobody answered
Every time that we tried
We're the only ones in the world
Who even knew that she died

They shut down the mill and no one is hanging around
She was the last stripper in the last club in town
I can't say that I knew her, I can't say we were friends
But I still call that number every now and then

Oh, but nobody answered
Every time that we tried
We're the only ones in the world
Who even knew that she died

NINE VOLT HEART
(R&B LOVE SONG TO TRANSISTOR RADIOS)
DAVE ALVIN / ROD HODGES

His momma said, "Baby, wait for me in the car"
Then she went lookin' for his daddy inside a bar
So he sat and let the radio take him far away
Listening to XPRS and KRLA

    Plastic silver nine volt heart
    You click it on and let the music start
    The radio was his toy
    The radio was his toy

Rachel was twenty and he was seventeen years old
Sittin' in a parked car on a country road
Runnin' his fingers through her long black hair
While The Staples were singing, "Baby, I'll take you there"

    Plastic silver nine volt heart
    You click it on and let the music start
    The radio was his toy
    The radio was his toy

Doin' the dishes long after midnight
Talkin' 'bout the evening news with his wife
Their baby wakes up and starts to cry
So they turn the radio on for his lullaby

    Plastic silver nine volt heart
    You click it on and let the music start
    The radio was his toy
    The radio was his toy

HELP YOU DREAM
(HONKY-TONK CHARMER
CLINGS TO HIS DREAMS)

Well, is this seat taken? Would mind some company?
You've been alone all evening; would you like to talk with me?
Do I come here often? You might say that I do
Is someone home waiting? I was just gonna ask you
'Cause you're the prettiest woman I think I've ever seen
And tonight, if you let me, I'd like to help you dream

Well, you've got the nicest brown eyes and a little girl's smile
You should have been in movies. You say you haven't heard that in a while
You sound just like Dolly, singing along with the radio
Do you know someplace quiet where both of us could go?
'Cause you're the prettiest woman I think I've ever seen
And tonight, if you let me, I'd like to help you dream

'Cause I think I know what it looks like
When you get back home
Maybe dreamin' is all that you've got left
But I could tell you sweet lies
Like you've never heard before
You see I haven't stopped dreamin' yet

Well, how about another drink? What's that? You gotta go home?
You say it's been nice talkin', then why are you leaving me alone?
'Cause you're the prettiest woman I think I've ever seen
And tonight, if you let me, I'd like to help you dream

Well, do I come here often? You might say that I do

A POEM FOR
MERLE HAGGARD

I was drinking beer with an old friend
One afternoon in a dark bar
In the north San Fernando Valley.

He had just moved back
To his mother's tract home in the Valley
From an apartment on New York's lower east side.

He did most of the talking.
The pressure of being a minor rock cult hero
Had given him alcohol and drug problems
Plus a nervous breakdown.
Or so he said.

As we drank in the rundown bar he went on about
　This fucking manager
　This fucking record company
　This fucking booking agent
　This fucking critic
　This fucking guitar player
　This fucking drummer
　This fucking girlfriend.

He was doing better now, he announced,
But it was going to take him some time to recover from it all.

A middle-aged man was sitting two stools down,
Drinking whiskey and beer.

As my friend was talking,
The older man got up, walked to the jukebox,
Dropped in two quarters and cued Merle Haggard's
"Going Where the Lonely Go" to play repeatedly.
As he sat back down
The older man gripped his hands
Around his drinks
And softly mouthed the lyrics along with Merle.
I could see that his hands were bloody
And wrapped in torn rags.

Barroom etiquette says
You should never bother a man drinking alone
Who is singing along with a sad song,
Especially one with bloody hands.
So I didn't.

My friend paid no attention to the older man
And went on about
   Another fucking manager
   Another fucking record company
   Another fucking booking agent
   Another fucking critic
   Another fucking guitar player
   Another fucking drummer
   Another fucking girlfriend.

It's been tough,
My friend said,
As the older man rubbed
His bloody hands and rags together.
It's been tough
But it should be better in time.

TULARE DUST: A SONGWRITERS' TRIBUTE TO MERLE HAGGARD, LINER NOTES
DAVE ALVIN / TOM RUSSELL, 1994

The music of Merle Haggard embodies a unique vision and spirit of independence. From its beginnings in the uncompromising, hard-edged California country sound, Haggard's legacy has grown to include a diverse array of influences and directions that make it one of the most important bodies of contemporary American musical work.

Haggard's classic songs have encompassed all styles and topics, from early California dust bowl stories ("Tulare Dust," "Hungry Eyes"), prison songs ("Sing Me Back Home," "Branded Man"), drinking songs ("Swingin' Doors," "The Bottle Let Me Down"), road songs ("White Line Fever," "Ramblin' Fever"), work songs, blues, swing tunes, and at least a hundred great love songs.

Detractors often bring up "Okie From Muskogee" or "Fightin' Side of Me" as evidence of exaggerated patriotism, but they've missed the point. Haggard's songs are the work of an uncompromising and honest writer. He may be the last of a breed of great country songwriters that began with Jimmie Rodgers and continued through Hank Williams and Lefty Frizzell.

This project wasn't conceived of as "the stars doing Merle's hits." It's just a group of acclaimed roots performers singing their favorite Merle song (the artists include Iris DeMent, Dwight Yoakam, Steve Young, Lucinda Williams, Billy Joe Shaver, Marshall Crenshaw, Joe Ely, Katy Moffatt, Robert Earl Keen, Peter Case, Rosie Flores, Barrence Whitfield, John Doe, Tom Russell and Dave Alvin). We mentioned the name "Haggard," and these writers said they'd love to be involved. As we listened back to the performances, we were moved by each singer's ability to get inside the Haggard song and make it his or her own.

Merle Haggard's recorded work and song catalogue insure his position as one of the most important singer-songwriter-musicians in modern American music. Go out and find the records. Listen to the songs. His kind ain't comin' 'round again.

HIGHWAY 99
(A LOVE SONG TO THE SAN JOAQUIN VALLEY)

Well, I woke up this morning in a one room apartment
On the east side of Nashville, Tennessee
Starin' out the window at a cold, gray morning
And wondering what had happened to me
I was feelin' like an old fool
Rememberin' a girl who
I knew in another lifetime
I left her waiting for me back home in California
In a small town off Highway 99
Well, I played every bar from Bakersfield to Modesto
Makin' just enough to get us by
Along that San Joaquin highway
I heard every drunk say, "Boy, go give Nashville a try"
Well, it's been three years or more here
Just gettin' nowhere
And more and more I ask myself why
I left her waitin' for me back home in California
In a small town off Highway 99

  Now the rain is falling on the trees and the houses
  On the east side of Nashville, Tennessee
  But in my mind the sun is shinin' down
  On oil fields and orchards spreading as far as I can see

And she's layin' there beside me, holdin' me tightly
With kisses sweet as grapes from the vine
I left her waitin' for me back home in California
In a small town off Highway 99

Now the rain is falling on the trees and the houses
On the east side of Nashville, Tennessee
But in my mind the sun is shinin' down
On oil fields and orchards spreading as far as I can see

And she's layin' there beside me, holdin' me tightly
With kisses sweet as grapes from the vine
I left her waitin' for me back home in California
In a small town off Highway 99

"JUST DON'T MENTION DON RICH"
INTRODUCTION TO THE *MIX* MAGAZINE INTERVIEW WITH BUCK OWENS

It was impossible not to notice the two neat stacks of twenty-dollar bills sitting on Buck Owens's coffee table. Each stack of cash was about six inches high and was placed on the table in front of the black leather couch where my friend Bruce Bromberg and I were directed by Jim Shaw to sit down. Jim was Buck's cordial yet protective piano player, band leader, and right-hand man.

After sitting down, I looked around at Buck's secret dressing room/apartment. If you were an audience member downstairs at Buck's Crystal Palace nightclub in Bakersfield, California, you'd have no idea that this deluxe private space existed directly above the stage. I glanced behind me at a small but full kitchen with an adjoining private dining area. Next to that was a bathroom and another door leading to what looked like a very nice bedroom. I watched as Jim Shaw walked away into the bedroom and closed the door behind him. I looked around at the living room where Bruce and I were seated. There was a large, very comfortable looking black leather reclining chair across from us and the coffee table with the two stacks of cash. A small gas fire was burning in the stone fireplace against the wall.

This elaborate dressing room was just like the man it belonged to, impressive and modern, yet still down to earth and traditional. Nothing too fancy or decadent, just all the comforts of home for a one-time Dust Bowl kid who grew up poor on Texas and Arizona farms. It perfectly suited an icon who struggled tirelessly at a music career until he became perhaps the most famous country singer in the world, as well as a highly influential hit-making machine—a beloved if sometimes outlandish entertainer, a syndicated television star, and a seriously shrewd businessman. His

189

private dressing room was exactly the sweet set up that most of us touring musicians fantasize about having at every gig, right down to the stacks of cash placed neatly on the coffee table.

Jim Shaw came out of the bedroom, walked over to me, and whispered in my ear, "Remember what I told you earlier. Just don't mention Don Rich. If Buck mentions Don Rich, then you can ask about Don, but if he doesn't, and you do ask about Don . . . well, he may just walk out of the interview." I nodded that I understood. I'd heard rumors that Buck had never quite recovered from Don's sudden, tragic death in a motorcycle accident more than twenty years earlier. Don Rich was a brilliant guitarist whose playing had influenced not only every country guitarist of the last 50 years, but even blues players like Roy Buchanan, as well as rock and rollers like George Harrison and Jerry Garcia. Don was also one of the architects of the West Coast / Bakersfield country sound along with Buck and Merle Haggard. But, perhaps most importantly, he was also Buck's trusted musical and creative soulmate. A legitimate case could even be made that with Rich's tight, evocative harmony vocals and his piercing, serpentine guitar licks on Buck's biggest hit records, Don Rich was as big a part of the "Buck Owens Sound" as Buck Owens ever was.

Jim Shaw smiled and added, "Just relax. Buck is one of the nicest guys in the world, very willing to discuss just about anything. Depending on how things go, he could talk for 30 minutes or 2 hours, so just follow where he leads you and enjoy the ride."

Then Buck Owens walked out of the bedroom, and I felt my heart rate kick into high gear. Jim did the introductions and, after shaking hands with us, Buck sat down in the recliner chair and removed his cowboy boots. He had just played a set with the current incarnation of his band, The Buckaroos. Instead of the show being a Buck Owens greatest hits affair, however, he stayed in the background, content to play lead guitar while other members of his band sang covers of country classics and newer Nashville hits. He wasn't advertised to perform that night and was only there to fill in for his lead guitarist who had to attend a funeral a few hours north in the town of Visalia. It was an incredibly rare treat to see Buck, liberated from his normal show business persona, simply being the guitar player in a country bar band. It was like when he first started out, decades before, as an unknown guitar slinger playing all night in honky tonks up and down central California's San Joaquin Valley before getting up early the next day to drive two hours over the treacherously mountainous Grapevine highway to make early morning recording sessions at Capitol Studios in Hollywood where he'd play guitar for Wanda Jackson, Tennessee Ernie Ford, Skeets McDonald, and many others. No one could say Buck Owens wasn't driven to succeed.

I thought about making a joke to Buck about the stacks of twenties but then thought better of it. Maybe he didn't realize the money had been sitting there, but he must have certainly seen it when he sat down. Why would someone leave that much cash laying out like that in the first place? Maybe it was simply money Buck owed Jim or Jim owed Buck. But then I thought maybe it was some sort of crazy test from the old music business payola days. Maybe Buck didn't trust this rock and roll guitar basher that had driven up from Los Angeles. Maybe it was a bribe to make sure I wrote something positive. Maybe he just wanted to see if I really was there to do an interview for *Mix* magazine, or if I was just some lunatic lowlife who'd grab the cash, bolt out of the dressing room, and run to score some speed on the unpaved back alleys of Oildale, the blue-collar neighborhood on the northern outskirts of Bakersfield? Jim Shaw knew a bit about who I was, but did Buck?

I was aware that Buck was a big fan of The Derailers, an Austin, Texas-based country-rock band I'd produced three albums for, and whose style was a loving update of Buck's classic 1960s Bakersfield Sound. I also knew that Buck and Dwight Yoakam were close pals, so maybe he knew that I'd written Dwight's hit song, "Long White Cadillac." But then I realized I was obsessing about the money and why it was on the table because I was actually just extremely nervous about meeting and interviewing a truly larger-than-life living legend of not only country music but of all American roots music.

Fortunately, Buck immediately put me at ease with his charm and easygoing manner. I'd brought my friend Bruce along to help keep me focused and to fill in any gaps in my country music knowledge. Bruce may be in the Blues Hall of Fame for his songwriting and record production legacy (he'd produced albums by blues legends like Lightnin' Hopkins and Johnny Shines, as well as younger blues artists like Robert Cray and Joe Louis Walker), but his first love was country music. When Bruce mentioned that he was an acquaintance of the lesser-known Bakersfield music pioneer Fuzzy Owen, Buck quickly relaxed and opened up on a wide range of subjects, just like Jim Shaw had predicted.

The interview was supposed to last only thirty minutes—and Buck was supposed to go back on stage—but we wound up talking for two hours, and he never rejoined his band downstairs. When the editors at *Mix* magazine chopped down our lengthy conversation to fit the space they'd allotted for the piece, they sadly left out my favorite quote from Buck. When I told him that, as a kid, I always considered his classic '60s hits like "Tiger by the Tail" and "Act Naturally" to be rock and roll records because I heard them on Top 40 pop radio alongside hits by Sam Cooke, The Beatles, The Shirelles, and The Beach Boys, Buck started laughing. He then bent close to me and softly confessed that his two biggest musical heroes, the two artists that inspired him the most, were the Western swing giant Bob Wills and . . . rock and roll wildman Little Richard. He laughed again and admitted that if he had said such a thing in the '50s or '60s or '70s, or even the '80s, that his country music career would have ended as soon as the words came out of his mouth.

When the two 60-minute cassettes I'd brought along for the interview were full, Bruce and I said goodbye to Buck and Jim. We drove south on Highway 99 past dairy farms and orange groves on a beautiful, warm California night. We headed for the old Grapevine highway across the mountains, the same one that the young Buck Owens had driven on so many nights decades before. We were high with adrenalin after our evening, so Bruce and I excitedly swapped our favorite quotes that Buck had said to us just like any other two gushing fans would do. When an insane kid speeding on a motorcycle dangerously passed my car on the right, I instantly thought about Don Rich. I congratulated myself for not slipping up due to nerves and callously asking Buck about Don. Then I thought about the suspicious stacks of cash on the coffee table and how I never figured out why or what they were there for. But I felt just fine about that. Sometimes it's all right to let a little mystery linger forever.

BUCK OWENS: FROM THE STREETS OF BAKERSFIELD

Alvin: Tell me about the early days, how you started out.

Owens: When I was a kid, I always tried to hang around where the people were who played music. My mother played the piano. Boy, she could swing. She was self-taught—one of those that had a great big, wonderful left hand that I always wished to hell I could have. She'd just make the whole little old place thunder. I used to marvel at the fact that she learned how to do that all by herself.

Myself, I used to always try to get the nearest I could to where the band was playing, from the time I was 14. I was a big old kid. I was 6 foot tall when I was 14. I looked like a bean pole. In Arizona, when I was 16, the guy that owned this bar where I used to go would let me fool around a little bit in his place and be around the musicians, and if they needed a cigarette, I was their man. I was handy and didn't cause any trouble, so I got to hang around.

Later, I played in the honky tonks. I was a disc jockey, too, and I played five or six years of the Elvis craze—all the labels looking for another Elvis. It's just like now they're all looking for another Garth. But I love what Chet Atkins said about today's records. He said, "To make it now, you got to have some boots and a hat." And I thought, "Yeah, okay, I have a hat." And then he says, ". . . and a tight ass."

Alvin: [Laughs] What do you think of today's country music? You obviously have a big stake in it because of your involvement in radio.

Owens: Raul [Malo] from The Mavericks—they were here [at the Crystal Palace] recently—we kind of have a mutual thing going. I just love their stuff because it's unafraid. He was saying—I think it was in yesterday's paper—that he was just lamenting the state of radio. Now, I'm in the radio business in a big-time way. I have three stations here, and I have four stations over in Phoenix: three country and one adult contemporary, and the morning program [on the adult contemporary one] happens to be the Number One program in town.

Alvin: In a way, aren't you kind of split, because on one hand you're a creative artist who's done revolutionary things, and on the other hand you're famous for being a very astute businessman. You're kind of caught between two worlds.

Owens: I have an answer for that: I'm not in the radio business; I'm in the advertising business. A lot of people don't realize how important Madison Avenue is to radio and TV. If we don't get the demographics as well as Madison Avenue in New York wants, then they can't sell us to Chevrolet, they can't sell us to Ford, they can't sell us to IBM. They can't sell it, and that's where you make your big money.

I have people like you who I like to hear. I'm a Little Richard fan. I'm a Bob Wills fan. Who are my influences, my first influences, outside of gospel aspect and the bluegrass aspect? There's a town in Arizona called Wiggleman. A little bitty town that had one store. We lived in Mountain Country, and my daddy had this old car radio. We had a '31 Model A, and this is 1938. He had this car radio, and it had this dial that you turned that went all the way around the radio, but we didn't have to turn it much, because there were only two stations you could get. They were these big, powerful AMs from Mexico. I remember them like it was yesterday. One was way over on the righthand side, and one was at 800, and they'd play all these acetates that these guys would cut: Bill and Charlie Monroe, and Wayne and Lonnie Dawson. That's what they played late at night. Those were my early influences.

It's not easy being a broadcaster and being a musician. What I love about listening to the radio, about listening to music, is separate from the business side.

Alvin: Tell us about the early session.

Owens: Okay. You guys ever heard of [songwriter / recording artist] Stan Freeberg?

Alvin: Oh, yeah.

Owens: Well, this was on one of his sessions. Jack Marshall, who was the guitar player who used to play all the movie music, he was the bandleader on this particular session. This was about '54. He had ten of us in there: A piano player named . . . I can't think of his name right now . . . he was from San Diego.

Bromberg: Merrill Moore?

Owens: Yeah, you got it! My God, how'd you think of him? Just a great, wonderful touch on the piano—a great left hand.

Bromberg: He's still going, did you know that? Still playing.

Owens: No! Still in San Diego?

Bromberg: Yeah.

Owens: If you see him somehow, tell him to call me. But I want to tell you this story. They gave us music. Well, I read music a little bit. I taught myself to read some music, and I can pick out the notes a little bit, but not good enough to sight read. The music had an e-flat diminished with a suspended fifth. [Laughter] Well, I was about from here to there where Merrill was sitting, and I asked him, "Okay if I scoot over there? I'd kind of like to, I'm hearing some kind of harmonic or something here." [Laughs] He said, "Sure." Of course, you couldn't just do that in those days. You had to have the engineer move you over. So I go over next to Merrill, and he's an old country boy, you know, so I said to Merrill, "What the hell do you make of this suspended fifth stuff?" And he said, "Well, we gotta find out which one's the fifth." [More laughter] He said to me, "Is there a diminished scale?" And I said, "I'm diminishing sitting here right now." But he could read good enough to do the chords, and what he didn't know, it didn't take me long to figure it out. Those were the fun times, playing on sessions. Most of the time, I'd drive back and work at night, too, though, because at 23 years old you don't feel anything.

Alvin: What was that like? You'd work in Bakersfield or the Valley honky tonks, then have to be [in LA] at 9 AM sessions?

Owens: Right. I'd just drive down there. They never started before 10 down there, most times not till 1. And we'd be working, and then who comes in but Frank Sinatra or Kennedy's brother-in-law—Peter Lawford—and next thing you know, Stan's leaving with them—they're out going into the other studio, and I'm just sitting around thinking it's the most I ever made on a record. Ten hours at that time paid like 120 bucks. Well, you know, I'm talking like 1954.

Alvin: One thing I was curious about was, do you remember the Gene Vincent sessions?

Owens: Yeah, I remember. The main song we did over there was [sings] "Well, I wanna wanna lotta lotta lovin'…"

Alvin: You were on that? Wow!

Owens: Yeah. By that time, I was writing some songs, too, and I was doing some new things on a little bitty label called Pep. The guy who ran it, his entire record label was his bedroom. He had a little desk, and, you know, where's the rest of it? I'm sure it was tough, but somehow it seems like it was more fun then. It wasn't easy, because I tell you the big difference between cutting now and cutting then is that, if the three of us go in and play, we would make some kind of cut. But everybody on those sessions was not always what I'd call adequate. Sometimes there was somebody on the session because they were a brother-in-law or something, and you'd get all the way up to the end, or two-thirds of the way through, and someone makes a mistake. You had to go all the way back to the top.

On my own records, I always used my own band. And I did that for a reason—not just because they were all good musicians. I did that because I didn't want to sound like everybody.

Alvin: With a lot of the bands that I work with when I produce, and when I make my own records, the latest trend is to do it live, the old-fashioned way. And I was curious about the way you recorded in that classic period. When you made "Tiger by the Tail," "Together Again," your vocals were live, right?

Owens: They all were live, yeah. What we would do, though, when we would have three tracks, we would save a track for the harmony vocal, because I was real sticky about harmony. I can't recall ever doing just a vocal in those days. After we got to 8-track—I didn't get to 8-track myself until '67 or early '68, but once I got there, I liked it, because man it gave us so much more space.

Bromberg: Who sang the harmony on "Excuse Me"?

Owens: I did. [sings] "Excuse me . . ." and I split the harmony off and went into the high part. I never liked to sing like a fifth against a first or a first against a fifth. Layering sometimes was why I made those little different harmonies.

Alvin: Now, let's talk about Ken Nelson. Not to say he discovered you, but you fell in with him pretty early on as a session musician.

Owens: Yeah. The way I got in with Ken Nelson was because of Ferlin Husky. He got a big hit in '53 with Jean Shepherd called "Dear John Letter." It was a million-seller, and so they got a chance to go on a tour. He had played with Tommy Collins, so he called me up the night he was leaving and said, "Could you go down tomorrow and play on Tommy's session? I forgot to get somebody," and Ken was the producer on Tommy's session. The first record he had didn't do anything, I don't think, but the second one was "You Better Not Do That," and then "What You Gonna Do Now?"

Alvin: You played on those?

Owens: Yeah, that's me. That's how I got in with Ken. And Ken remembers it one way, and I never dispute it, but I'll tell you this: I read on several different occasions where he's said I bugged him to death. But I never did even ask him about recording for his label. He knew what I was—although I don't think he was real familiar with my singing—but I was doing a lot of sessions for him, and I didn't want to mess that up by hounding him about recording Buck.

But Ken might have been the best producer for a person like me, for a person like Merle [Haggard], for a person like Hank Thompson, who have our own bands and our own songs. I'd see Ken Nelson sit there with a pad and a pencil, and all he'd do was doodle. Every once in a while, he'd say, "You there," and that used to be me sometimes, and he'd say, "Ah, ah, are you in tune? Is that string in tune?" And I'd say, "Uh, let me check that, Mr. Nelson." He was so smart. He never injected himself into these records.

I guess I became kind of his fair-haired boy; if you ever talk to him, he'll tell you. He liked the fact that I came on time, that I was dressed, I was ready, I was talented, I brought my guitars, that I had a lot of nerve, and lot of ideas—preposterous as they were sometimes, he'd say.

I worked on a lot of his sessions that I got credit for being on and got paid for; I might not even have played a note, but when you look on there it was Buck Owens guitar, Buck Owens ukulele, Buck Owens banjo. Or Buck Owens drums! With Jean Shepherd one time—now this was before the multi-tracks—they had a little syncopation on the song "I Used to Love Him." It would go, [sings] "I Used to love him but I don't—bam—anymore," but the drummer couldn't keep the beat. He stopped the beat to do that "bam," and the whole thing would stop just about, and Ken says to me, "Can you play something there?" and I said, "Well, yeah, I guess. What would you like me to play?" And he said, "Hell, if I knew that, I'd tell ya. That's why you're here." And I said, "Yes, sir," and I made this little sound with sticks and a pillow that made a kind of whack, and he said, "That's what I mean, why don't you play that?"

Or there was a time when we was recording, and he'd say, "Damn, we need a ukulele. Uh, Buck, can you play ukulele?" I said, "Well, I never have, but it's got strings on it, maybe I could." So he holds out a $20 bill and he says, "There's a music store down here, the one nearest to the tower, go get us a ukulele. I think it's $11. A little plastic ukulele." I'd been around a ukulele, although I don't think I'd ever had played one, but I knew that it was tuned like the last four strings of the guitar, so I figured it out. Those were the fun days. Those were the creative days, the carefree days.

Alvin: Let's talk about some of your work in TV.

Owens: I did a television show called The Buck Owens Ranch Show, which I think there's about 400 [episodes] of. We use them here [at the Crystal Palace club] often. Some people in New York are interested, I might syndicate it. It's a seller because you got a lot of people on there, from Waylon [Jennings] to Roy Clark to Jimmy Dean.

Alvin: I grew up watching that show. Were those filmed here in Bakersfield?

Owens: No, they were filmed in Oklahoma City at WKY—the same people who owned Hee Haw. I own all the masters. I got all the masters for my albums, too.

Bromberg: That's amazing for that time.

Alvin: How did you do that?

Owens: There was this guy who was running the department then [at Capitol], and he and his business lawyer came to Reno while I was appearing; it was 1970. I'd never heard about anybody ever having their masters at that time; the record companies owned them forever.

So I told my attorney to tell [Capitol] that tomorrow the contract is up, and Clive Davis has offered me a half a million dollars signing bonus with Columbia. That deal was kind of a mess, and I don't think I would have ever signed with them anyway, but that is another story. And so I told them first thing I wanted all my material back, everything, and then we'll talk about a record deal. I said don't come if that's not a deal; then we'll work out the other. I worked out a five-year contract, and they would have a five-year sell-off, and then I would get everything back. So, it would be ten years from then before I got the catalog, but I'd get it all complete.

For a long time, I didn't think about it being such a big deal. I just left them in there. Once in a while, there'd be a movie thing—a guy comes along with ten grand—and then I'd get them. But otherwise, we didn't do anything until about 1990. Then I started taking things out, and I leased ten albums all at once to Toshiba over in Japan. I got $50,000 guaranteed from Toshiba, and then along comes this guy from up in New York, with [the label] Sundazed, and I get $100,000, and then I did all these little things with Time Warner, so we're averaging about $420,000 a year—of course, there's about 65 or 70 albums in there, too.

Alvin: That's a lot of material.

Owens: In those days, there'd be years you'd have three or four albums; they'd put out an album every three or four months. And [after the sessions], if you had a little time left over, you'd cut another song. I cut a song called "Buckaroo" when we had 15 minutes left over of a session. I'd say, "Any of you guys got something we can cut?" Because I knew that once I had ten instrumentals, one of these days, I'd release them. So [at one time] I had an instrumental album, and I had a religious album, and I had a Christmas album, and I had three other albums out; I had six albums out in six months' time. The labels didn't care, and I thought the more the merrier. So, I ended up with about 70 albums over the period of 18 years I was with Capitol.

Alvin: One of the reasons you're successful and you're a legend is—and this has to do with when you were discussing your influences, Little Richard and Bob Wills—Buck Owens is everything to everybody. To country people, you're a country singer, and I know to me growing up you were a rock 'n' roll singer, because I heard you on the radio with rock 'n' roll.

Owens: People still say that to me, "You were a rock guy," and I tell them, "No. Wait a minute now. Don't get me in bad," because none of the country charts . . . if they thought that you were trying to get a record played on a rock station, they resented it something terrible. That's why when I had a song like this, [sings in a rock 'n' roll voice] "Hot dog, she's my baby . . ." I put it out under a different name, Corky Jones.

Alvin: There was an aggressive side to your records. I don't mean hard rock, but in the guitar solos—in the fact that at the same time Nashville was doing the strings and the choruses, you guys were basically a rock 'n' roll band.

Owens: We were rockin', yeah. But the Nashville people didn't want me to say I was a Little Richard fan. They wanted me to say I was an Ernest Tubb fan. And I was an Ernest Tubb fan. But my influences weren't all country. I worked at this club over here for almost eight years called the Blackboard. It held 500 people. It was a big old club; they built onto it three or four times, and the way I kept that job was I learned [sings part of "Long Tall Sally"] and things like that, because I got requests for it. I learned all those songs that people wanted to hear. And the Bob Wills things, I knew most of those before I came here, but [I'd take] the Bob Wills thing and put a little Little Richard drive to it. That's where that came from, the aggressive guitar licks and solos.

Alvin: Well, and even when you used Mel Taylor on drums.

Owens: Yeah, Mel Taylor, what a guy. Well, at the time I didn't have a drummer, and I knew The Ventures because I'd spent two years up in Washington, and a couple of those boys were from up there. So I called him up and asked him. He did the little thing like on "My heart . . . [sings a drum roll] skips a beat . . ."

Alvin: That was pretty controversial, that one drum lick.

Owens: Yeah, that one little simple thing. I remember I got a note from a guy who said the guitar and the drums were too loud on my records. He wasn't buying any more until I got it right. I even wrote the guy a letter. I was very conscientious about wanting to do the right thing with the fans, because I've been in a cotton field. I knew what it was like.

Alvin: I'm curious about the different country styles of country music. Obviously, there are differences between the West Coast / Bakersfield country sound and the Nashville sound. Nashville seems like a monolithic town that people like you and Merle and Lefty Frizzell and some other people have always had problems with. What do you think of Nashville and the shape of country music now?

Owens: How much time have you got? [Laughs] I tell you what, I'll tell you this little story about a manager going in to the record company and saying, "I got a boy that you're going to like." The guy at the record company will say, "Well, what's he look like? Good looking boy?" "Yeah, he's a good looking boy." "How tall is he?" "Oh, he's 6 foot." "Does he wear a hat and boots?" "Oh, he looks great in them." "Is he married?" "No." "How old is he?" "He's 23." "Well, okay, you got a deal," and they shake hands, and the manager goes over to the door, and the guy says, "Oh, wait, by the way, can he sing?" That's the last thing they ask.

Alvin: Well, it kind of brings us back full-circle to what we started off talking about. You were saying you're in the advertising business when you talk about the radio side of your career, and it seems like it's so much easier to sell things that all sound the same. But in the '60s / early '70s, Buck Owens and Merle Haggard were the Bakersfield sound, and you didn't sound alike, and neither of you sounded anything like Nashville country.

Owens: I have a reason for that, and that is, see, out here, you couldn't make a nickel if you couldn't play for a dance. So we had drums in our groups, and we used to play more of a dance sound than they did, because down there in the South, it's too much of a sin to be dancing and rubbing your body up against some gal's body. That's sinful.

Alvin: You know, I never thought of that. That is the biggest difference between the Eastern style of country music and the Western. You're right.

Owens: Yeah. Dancing is always a bit more aggressive. I never liked the syrupy sickening feeling of some of those songs. Though I recognize the talent of some of those people that came from there, I would have liked to have heard them with a different sound. I just wonder what would have happened—if they thought I was pretty raw—what if Steve Earle had come along about that time?

BLUES FOR BRUCE BROMBERG

I first saw Bruce Bromberg's name when I was a 12-year-old kid in 1968, on the back covers of some blues reissue albums he'd produced and written the liner notes for. Little did I know then that he and I would someday become close friends, co-conspirators, and musical partners.

In the early 1970s I saw his name credited as producer for new recordings by Lightnin' Hopkins, Johnny Shines, Lonesome Sundown, Phillip Walker, and other blues masters. In the 1980s, I saw his name again listed as producer of artists like Robert Cray, Jimmie Dale Gilmore, and Joe Louis Walker for the Hightone Records label that he co-owned with his best friend, Larry Sloven. Bruce's many years of record producing and songwriting were why he was rightfully inducted into the Blues Hall of Fame.

When I signed with Hightone in 1990, Bruce became my record producer / career advisor, and we quickly turned into tight, lifelong comrades (even after I left Hightone in 2003). He and I shared great times together, whether it was in the recording studio, drinking beers in dive bars, traveling through the South searching for the graves of blues titans, hanging out with rockabilly legends Sonny Burgess, Roland Janes, and Billy Lee Riley, or spending a memorable evening in Bakersfield with Buck Owens discussing Bob Wills and Little Richard.

Bruce was a wise, opinionated, soulful, and very funny man who I could always count on to be there for me in times of heartbreak, loss, and pain. Today I heard that Bruce passed away at 80 years old after enduring a long, brutal battle with Alzheimer's disease. As silly as it sounds, I wish I could call Bruce now or meet him at Rae's greasy spoon on Pico for lunch like I had for decades. I know he would have easily made me laugh at life's absurdities and gotten me through the deep sadness I'm feeling right now.

Thank you for your life of music, laughter, and everything you did for me, my dear old friend. Whatever lies on the other side, Bruce, I'll find you there, and the beers and all the tunes on the jukebox will be on me.

ROMEO'S ESCAPE
(LUST AT INDIANAPOLIS SPEEDWAY TEMPO)

Well, in a bar in an oil town on the bayou I can't say
She made herself a vow to drink her whole life away
She shows the barkeep an old photo
Says, "Have you seen my darling Romeo?"

Well, there's a big, busty blonde in Oklahoma City
Sittin' in front of a mirror just making herself pretty
She thinks she's meetin' Romeo at half-past eight
But Romeo left town on a southbound freight

  Yeah, Romeo, Romeo,
  Wherefore art thou and where did you go?
  You've got all these chicks just moanin' low
  For their Romeo, their little Romeo

Well, now in a New York apartment she's with her rich boyfriend
And he's tellin' her it's true love that will never end
But as he's braggin' 'bout all things he's gonna get her
All she really wants is sweet Romeo's letter

Well, in Cheyenne, Wyoming, deer and antelope roam
And a pretty little cowgirl took a lonesome stranger home
Some will call it love, some will call it hate
But she ain't never kissed nobody since Romeo escaped

  Whoa, Romeo, Romeo,
  Wherefore art thou and where did you go?
  You've got all these women just moanin' low
  For their Romeo, their little Romeo

Well, I was tryin' to kiss my baby, you know, the one I love the best
She said, "Hang on, Dave, I gotta get somethin' off my chest"
I said, "Baby, what are you tryin' to say?"
She said, "I hate to tell you, Dave, but Romeo was here today"

Yes, Romeo, Romeo,
Wherefore art thou and where did you go?
You've got all these women just moanin' low
For their Romeo, their little Romeo

PLASTIC ROSE
(A JAZZ BALLAD FOR CONFUSED COUPLES)

From a vase on a coffee shop table
Mary picked herself a flower
While I called a number on a business card
And they said, "Call back in an hour"
So I sat back down next to Mary
And I said, "You shouldn't eat I suppose"
But Mary didn't say anything to me
She just held a plastic rose

"You two look so sweet," the waitress said
"So when is the lucky day?"
Well, I ordered a Coke and I tried to smile
Until the waitress went away
"Do you think she knew?" Mary said
"Do you think that it really shows?"
Then she folded her hands in her lap
And she held a plastic rose

   And I feel like I should say something
   But what? Well, I don't know
   When I offer her my hand, she turns away
   And she holds a plastic rose

I smoked my last cigarette
As I watched the clock on the wall
Mary didn't say anything to me
When I said it was time to call

But we'd talked about it for a week
Both agreeing in what we chose
So I called a number on a business card
And she held a plastic rose

  And I feel like I should say something
  But what? Well, I don't know
  When I offer her my hand, she turns away
  And she holds a plastic rose

PATERNITY TEST

I was working on my hillside trimming cactus when two women in their twenties passed by walking their small dogs on the dead-end road behind my property. A minute or so later they walked back and gestured towards me while smiling and whispering to each other.

"Excuse me, sir. Sorry to bother you but could you answer a question for us?"

"Sure," I said as I stood up to face them on the other side of my fence.

"Well, uh, are you Kid Rock's dad?" Said one of the young women. "We've seen you around the neighborhood and we thought you two looked so much alike that you might be his dad," the second woman explained.

I was more than a little stunned by their question. Then I thought about how I looked. I was wearing an old straw fedora, a pair of Ray Charles–style Ray-Ban sunglasses, and my long, pandemic hair was hanging down around my face.

"Why . . . yes, I am," I said with a straight face as I walked closer to them.

"Wow. That's so cool. We heard a rumor that Kid Rock bought his dad a house around here," the second woman said. "We're not big fans of his or anything. We just thought it was nice of him to buy you a house."

I didn't bother telling them that the real father of Kid Rock was actually a multi-millionaire who owned several car dealerships in Michigan, or the fact that Kid Rock didn't grow up in a Midwest trailer park despite his carefully crafted stage persona.

"Yeah, we were just curious. We're really sorry to bother you," the first woman said. Then, after a moment of awkward silence, she added, "You must be really proud of him." She paused and confessed, "To be honest, though, I don't like his music at all."

"Neither do I," I answered. "In fact, I hate it more than you ever could, but it got me a home and this hillside full of cactus plants so I can't complain much."

"Well, it was really nice of him to do that for you," the second woman said.

"Yes, it was," I said as they started to walk away. "But the bum never calls me."

I'm a big fan of telling and hearing the truth. It's very important that politicians, news outlets, law enforcement, friends, relatives, partners, guitar bashers, etc., all tell us the truth. But sometimes it's a nice guilty kick to lie a little when the lie is meaningless and harmless. The hard truth and reality for me, though, is that I must come to grips with the disturbing fact that I just may look like Kid Rock or his dad.

COMMON GROUND
LINER NOTES

Brothers fight sometimes. They argue, tease, bully, and disagree. Some-times they even fight when they agree. But brothers are also brothers. A brother will teach you, guide you, protect you, and even learn from you. He'll make you proud or make you laugh like no one else or get you into or out of trouble. Some folks say there is an unbreakable, almost mystical bond between siblings that no amount of arguing or disagreement can shatter. They say no matter how mad you are at your brother, no matter how thin the mystical bond is stretched by fate or circumstance, wherever you go, whatever you do, your brother is always your brother. I can't speak for anyone else but, in my experience, that is the damn truth.

I distinctly remember the day when my brother Phil brought home our first Big Bill Broonzy record. It was a reissue album of some of Big Bill's late 1930s recordings titled *Big Bill's Blues*. I was 13 and Phil was 15, and we considered ourselves pretty musically hip. Thanks to our older cousins Donna Dixon, Mike Keller, and Joe Alvin Jr.'s eclectic tastes in music, we'd been exposed to rhythm and blues, folk, doo-wop, rock and roll, soul, surf, country, and even pure blues (we already had albums by Sonny Boy Williamson, Lightnin' Hopkins, Sonny Terry and Brownie McGhee), but when we heard Big Bill's powerful yet friendly voice; his nuanced, confident guitar playing; and his lyrically vivid, tough songs, my brother and I were hooked.

Unlike more mysterious, obscure blues performers who cut a few records then disappeared, Big Bill had a long, diverse recording career stretching 30 years from the late 1920s to the late '50s. He recorded in a variety of blues styles and formats, from his early solo acoustic guitar masterpieces to swinging with uptown horn combos, from hard-edged harmonica/piano-driven Chicago stompers to his late career return to acoustic, traditional folk music and razor-sharp songs about race and class relations. Big Bill defied genres but still always sounded like Big Bill Broonzy. Along with Woody Guthrie, Leadbelly, and the Carter Family, it's almost impossible to imagine modern American folk music without Big Bill's contribution. He and his songs influenced everyone from rural and urban blues performers to country swing bands, folk music purists, rhythm and blues shouters, British and American folk, skiffle and blues/rock musicians, and then all the way to two young brothers in Downey, California.

After that first day we heard Big Bill, as my brother and I went out on our passionate teenage explorations of junk stores, swap meets, and dingy attics searching for old, dusty, and scratchy 78s and 45s, we were always on the lookout for more of his records. Not much changed over the decades. Through years of growing up together, making music together and not making music together, through times of success, disappointment, disagreement, tragedy, distance, triumph and closeness, Big Bill Broonzy remained, in many ways our shared musical square one. Our common ground.

WHAT'S UP WITH YOUR BROTHER?
(ETERNAL SIBLING BLUES)

Dave Alvin:
I've been fightin' this guitar over 30 long years
'Til there's blood on my hands and ringing in my ears
I sing my songs 'round the world, one end to the other
But all anyone asks is, "What's up with your brother?"

Phil Alvin:
I catch rattlesnakes with my bare hands
Sang jazz with Sun Ra, played in T-Bone Walker's band
I'll debate time and space and the theory of numbers
But all anyone asks is, "What's up with your brother?"

   DA: You can run, you can hide but you'll soon discover
   PA: No matter where you run blood is thicker than water
   TOGETHER: No one asks about our father, sister, or mother
   All they ever ask is, "What's up with your brother?"

DA: I could have money in my pockets or not a dime to my name
PA: Whether I'm drunk or sober, you know it's always the same
PA: Might be the cop on the beat
DA: It might be some little lover
TOGETHER: All anyone asks is, "What's up with your brother?"

DA: Now, when the time comes to meet our final fate
PA: Some say the fires of hell, some say the pearly gates
DA: Well, I don't give a damn one way or another
TOGETHER: 'Cause all they're gonna ask is, "What's up with your brother?"

PA: You can run, you can hide
DA: But you'll soon discover
PA: No matter where you run blood is thicker than water
TOGETHER: No one asks about our father, sister or mother
All they ever ask is, "What's up with your brother?"

All they ever ask is
"What's up with your brother?"

SOUTHWEST CHIEF
(FOR CHARLIE, SARAH, AND THE ROOTS ON THE RAILS TRIBE)
DAVE ALVIN / BILL MORRISSEY

Leaving Chicago on the Southwest Chief
Past old brick houses on bootlegger streets
I snuck outside the last coach to the cold Midwest wind
I light up a smoke and feel alive again

  Southwest Chief, let your whistle blow
  Wherever you're headed I want to go

Racin' through cornfields and nameless small towns
Porch lights comin' on as the sun goes down
Folks I've known and loved keep crossin' my mind
As the train keeps on pushin' and makin' up lost time

I remember my friend Bill Morrissey
We were gonna write a song but that was never to be
"Make it a blues," he said, "sweet and tough yet sincere
'Cause we only come 'round once and then we disappear"

  Southwest Chief, let your whistle blow
  Wherever you're headed I want to go

Kansas City has lightning, Colorado has rain
All the simple things in life are so hard to explain
Like your very first kiss, burning hot as any flame
Or watching the world speeding by from the back of a train

Crossing New Mexico through a dusting of snow
Then on to Arizona and the land of the Navajo
I say some old prayer I learned as a child
For the helpless, the hopeless, the damned and the wild

Southwest Chief, let your whistle blow
Wherever you're headed I want to go

I left Chicago on the Southwest Chief
Riding steel wheels and searchin' for some kind of peace
Sweet California is waiting at the end of the line
But I may just jump back on and ride you one more time

Southwest Chief, let your whistle blow
Wherever you're headed I want to go

SPRINGFIELD, ILLINOIS, OCTOBER 12, 2015

I spent last night in a rundown motel in downtown Springfield, Illinois.
The fading, mid-20th century motel was a half block from
The 19th century home of tragic poet, Vachel Lindsay.
Known as "The Prairie Troubadour,"
Mr. Lindsay was born on the first floor of the house in 1879.
And, after a life of hoboing, writing, acclaim, and hard luck,
He committed suicide on the second floor 52 years later.

Sometime after 2 AM, I stepped outside my dingy room for a smoke
And decided to walk down the dark alley to his house.
A prairie wind blew through old trees, a police siron cried nearby
And a slow freight train clanked through town just two streets away.
It was a perfect haunted night,
In a city already deeply haunted by the ghost
Of its adopted son (and Mr. Lindsay's hero) Abraham Lincoln,
To stare at a house doomed to eternal mourning.

I thought about walking the three empty, forlorn blocks
Over to Lincoln's old house but I decided against it.
Even though I don't believe in ghosts or such things,
Standing in the dark beneath the sad, somber windows
Of Mr. Lindsay's house late on an eerie night in a lonesome town,
I'll admit I did believe in that sort of thing for more than a moment or two.

SOMEWHERE IN TIME
(FINDING PEACE IN THE UNKNOWABLE)
DAVE ALVIN / LOUIE PEREZ / DAVID HIDALGO

I hear a voice, singing somewhere in time
  A song I knew long ago
And it takes me back, to places somewhere in time
  And everyone I used to know
I see a face I remember somewhere in time,
  Someone I knew who's gone away
Gone away somewhere in time
Gone away somewhere in time

Another night, on a highway somewhere in time,
  The darkness playing tricks on me
Far down the road in the shadows somewhere in time
  Am I the man I'm supposed to be?
I see a light shining somewhere in time
  A lonely light to lead me on
Lead me on somewhere in time
Lead me on somewhere in time

I wake from a dream, a dream from somewhere in time,
  And rub my eyes so I can see
You're standing there before me somewhere in time
  Waiting for me patiently
Then I'll take your hand someday somewhere in time
  And forever I'll be here with you
I'll be with you somewhere in time
I'll be with you somewhere in time
I'm here with you somewhere in time

(I WON'T BE) LEAVING
(LATE NIGHT BALLAD FOR JERRY BUTLER)

Well, it's cold and it's raining, the midnight cars roll down the street
Streetlights shine in the gutter, and you've gone off to sleep

    But, baby, I sit up smoking, wipe the ashes off the bed
    Think of what you told me and the words I've never said
    I won't be leavin', I won't be leavin' anymore

Now, police helicopters fly circles in the sky
And I ask myself, baby, could you believe just one more lie

    I sit up smoking, wipe the ashes off the bed
    Think of what you told me and the words I've never said
    I won't be leavin', I won't be leavin' anymore

    And I see you sleeping, our shoes on the floor
    And it'd be so easy, baby, to slip out the door
    But if you were awake, girl, I swear I would tell you
    That I won't be leavin' anymore

I hear sirens in the darkness tell sad stories in the night
It could have been me caught red-handed, could've been me who lost the
fight

    Baby, I sit up smoking, wipe the ashes off the bed
    Think of what you told me and the words I've never said
    I won't be leavin', I won't be leavin' anymore
    I won't be leavin', won't be leavin' anymore
    I won't be leavin', won't be leavin'

FOR THE REST OF MY LIFE

Though the recent hot days have been terribly brutal, the warm evenings have a sweet magic all their own. They have the sort of intoxicating appeal that made me sneak out of my parents' house after my bedtime when I was a pre-teen and ride my bike down the dark neighborhood streets, perhaps a few more blocks than my folks would ever have allowed.

My favorite memory of one of these warm evenings, after a day of desert heat, happened when I was 15 years old. My brother and some of the older guys had "rustled up" someone's old flatbed work truck in order to get us the 22 miles from Downey up to the Ash Grove because, goddamn, Freddie King was playing that night. There was no way we were going to miss that.

My brother Phil, Johnny Bazz, and the guy who was driving the truck sat crammed in the truck's front cab while the other older guys (Gene Taylor, Tom DeMott, Mike Kennedy, and Doug Allgood) and I clung to the exposed flatbed in the back of the truck. We pressed our backs against the truck cab's cool metal shell for some sense of security while our hands tried to grip the old, wooden slats of the floorboard to keep us from flying off each time the truck turned a corner. When we got on the freeway and the truck started getting up to some serious speed, Doug put his large arm around me and said, "Don't worry. I'll make sure you don't fly off. Shit, your brother would kill me if I let anything bad happen to you."

Somehow, one of the older guys managed to light a joint despite the hot, high-speed winds swirling madly around us. They passed the joint around to each other and it eventually made its way to me. I had never even smoked a regular cigarette before, let alone a marijuana one, but I took a short, tentative drag off the joint and tried to look cool. The older guys laughed and then taught me the proper technique for inhaling the herb. Not long after that, filled with teenage immortality from the weed, mixed with the exhilarating wind blowing through our hair and clothes, we were fearlessly standing up on the flatbed of the truck. We screamed and howled in excitement and joy like the small-town boys we truly were as the truck sped by the high-rise buildings of downtown Los Angeles and the mysterious side streets of Hollywood. I stared up at the cloudless summer sky and thought, "I want to feel like this for the rest of my life."

We got to the Ash Grove just in time to watch Freddie King hit the stage and start his set with his 1961 instrumental "San-Ho-Zay." This was a couple of years before Freddie was discovered by the rock music crowd, so his Ash Grove performance was still a chitlin' circuit show that was mainly the same set of brilliant King Records classics he'd been barnstorming for years. Mr. King was magnificent, to say the least. When he dug into his guitar on the rhythmic, repetitive "San-Ho-Zay" melodic riff, he nailed me to my seat, and I once again thought, "I want to feel like this for the rest of my life."

In some ways I have. I may have quit smoking weed a year or two after that ride in the back of the truck, and I may not recklessly expose myself to physical danger just for kicks anymore like on the flatbed that night, but I've luckily managed to have a career playing the music I love, and I've somehow survived doing just that. I also thankfully managed to keep alive inside me a bit of the rush of riding on the back of that truck through all the years that have passed since. No matter where in the world I'm performing, or what band I'm playing with, or whatever the musical style is, or what the volume levels are, I always throw in Mr. King's riff from "San-Ho-Zay" somewhere in the set, whether it works or not musically with the song I'm playing. I do this not only as a tribute to Mr. King but also as a tribute to warm summer evenings and to howling at the universe from the back of an old speeding truck while high on freedom and immortality.

BASIC DAVE ALVIN DISCOGRAPHY

SOLO ALBUMS:

FROM AN OLD GUITAR: RARE AND UNRELEASED
  RECORDINGS
Yep Roc Records, 2020

DOWNEY TO LUBBOCK (with Jimmie Dale Gilmore)
Yep Roc Records, 2018

LOST TIME (with Phil Alvin)
Yep Roc Records, 2015

COMMON GROUND: DAVE AND PHIL ALVIN PLAY THE
  SONGS OF BIG BILL BROONZY
Yep Roc Records, 2014

ELEVEN ELEVEN
Yep Roc Records, 2011

DAVE ALVIN AND THE GUILTY WOMEN
Yep Roc Records, 2009

THE BEST OF THE HIGHTONE YEARS
Hightone Records, 2008

LIVE FROM AUSTIN, TX: AUSTIN CITY LIMITS
New West Records, 2007

WEST OF THE WEST
Yep Roc Records, 2006

THE GREAT AMERICAN MUSIC GALAXY (LIVE)
Yep Roc Records 2005

ASHGROVE
Yep Roc Records, 2004

OUT IN CALIFORNIA (LIVE)
Hightone Records, 2002

PUBLIC DOMAIN: SONGS FROM THE WILD LAND
Hightone Records, 2000

BLACKJACK DAVID
Hightone Records, 1998

INTERSTATE CITY (LIVE)
Hightone Records, 1996

KING OF CALIFORNIA
Hightone Records, 1994

MUSEUM OF HEART
Hightone Records, 1993

BLUE BLVD
Hightone Records, 1991

ROMEO'S ESCAPE
Epic Records, 1987

WITH THE BLASTERS:

GOING HOME: THE BLASTERS LIVE
Shout Factory Records, 2004

TROUBLE BOUND: THE BLASTERS LIVE
Hightone Records, 2002

TESTAMENT: THE COMPLETE SLASH RECORDINGS
Slash/Warner Bros. Records, 2002

THE BLASTERS COLLECTION
Slash/Warner Bros. Records, 1991

HARD LINE
Slash/Warner Bros. Records, 1985

NON FICTION
Slash/Warner Bros. Records, 1983

OVER THERE: LIVE AT THE VENUE
Slash/Warner Bros. Records, 1982

THE BLASTERS
Slash/Warner Bros. Records, 1981

AMERICAN MUSIC
Rollin' Rock Records, 1980

ACKNOWLEDGMENTS

My most sincere thanks to Scott B. Bomar and everyone at BMG Books, David Hirshland, Mary Elizabeth Zerkie, Nancy Sefton, Debra Cronin, Danny Bland, Stanley Wycoff, Christy McWilson, Greg Leisz, David Wykoff, Glenn Dicker, David Shaw, Joe Murray, Jack Rudy, Frank Lee Drennen, Terry Allen, Katy Moffatt, Randy Lewis and the *Los Angeles Times*, Joe Travers, Zappa Trust, *Mix* magazine, Rhino Records, The Blasters, The All-Nighters, The Guilty Men, The Guilty Women, The Guilty Ones, and all the musicians and singers who have performed my songs.